ADV

"This smart, accessible book will help therapists everywhere do better by their clients and it might even help them transform their own lives along the way."

—**Daniel H. Pink,** #1 *New York Times* bestselling author of *When, Drive,* and *A Whole New Mind*

"This unique book is a lyrical, passionate, beautifully written guide that marries the art of being in real relationships with fellow human beings to the science of effective psychotherapy. Highly engaging, highly inspiring, and highly recommended for aspiring and experienced therapists of all therapeutic orientations."

—**Laurie Heatherington, PhD,** Edward Dorr Griffin Professor of Psychology, Williams College, coauthor of *Therapeutic Alliances in Couple and Family Therapy*

"Many people believe creativity can't be taught, but in *Therapeutic Improvisation,* Alcée deftly pulls it off, illuminating the artistry that inspires the work we do as therapists."

—**Lori Gottlieb,** *New York Times* bestselling author of *Maybe You Should Talk To Someone: A Therapist, Her Therapist, and Our Lives Revealed*

"This is the book I wish I had as a young therapist. With copious analogies to music, film, drama, literature, and the visual arts, Alcée softens the new practitioner's bumpy ride from cerebral conceptualization to emotionally alive, clinical engagement. Having this book in one's library is like having a big brother, private tutor, coach, and cheerleader all in one place and always available."

—**Nancy McWilliams, PhD,** Rutgers Graduate School of Applied & Professional Psychology, author of *Psychoanalytic Diagnosis, Psychoanalytic Case Formulation, Psychoanalytic Psychotherapy,* and *Psychoanalytic Supervision*

Therapeutic Improvisation

THE NORTON SERIES ON INTERPERSONAL NEUROBIOLOGY

Louis Cozolino, PhD, Series Editor
Allan N. Schore, PhD, Series Editor, 2007–2014
Daniel J. Siegel, MD, Founding Editor

The field of mental health is in a tremendously exciting period of growth and conceptual reorganization. Independent findings from a variety of scientific endeavors are converging in an interdisciplinary view of the mind and mental well-being. An interpersonal neurobiology of human development enables us to understand that the structure and function of the mind and brain are shaped by experiences, especially those involving emotional relationships.

The Norton Series on Interpersonal Neurobiology provides cutting-edge, multidisciplinary views that further our understanding of the complex neurobiology of the human mind. By drawing on a wide range of traditionally independent fields of research—such as neurobiology, genetics, memory, attachment, complex systems, anthropology, and evolutionary psychology—these texts offer mental health professionals a review and synthesis of scientific findings often inaccessible to clinicians. The books advance our understanding of human experience by finding the unity of knowledge, or consilience, that emerges with the translation of findings from numerous domains of study into a common language and conceptual framework. The series integrates the best of modern science with the healing art of psychotherapy.

A Norton Professional Book

Therapeutic Improvisation

How to **STOP WINGING IT** and **OWN IT** as a Therapist

MICHAEL ALCÉE

W. W. NORTON & COMPANY
Independent Publishers Since 1923

This book is intended as a general information resource for professionals practicing in the field of psychotherapy and mental health. It is not a substitute for appropriate training or clinical supervision. Standards of clinical practice and protocol change over time. No technique or recommendation is guaranteed to be safe or effective in all circumstances, and neither the publisher nor the author can guarantee the accuracy, efficacy, or appropriateness of any particular recommendation in every respect.

The names and identifying details of clients, supervisees, and any other individuals referenced in clinical sessions have been changed, quotations have been fictionalized, and some client cases are composites. Any URLs displayed in this book link or refer to websites that existed as of press time. The publisher is not responsible for, and should not be deemed to endorse or recommend, any website, app, or other content that it did not create. The author, also, is not responsible for any third-party material.

Sections from Chapter 1 appeared originally in Michael D. Alcée & Tara A. Sager (2017). How to Fall in Love With Time-Limited Therapy: Lessons From Poetry and Music, Journal of College Student Psychotherapy. Reprinted by permission of the publisher (Taylor & Francis Ltd, http://www.tandfonline.com).

For information about permission to reproduce selections from this book, write to Permissions, W. W. Norton & Company, Inc., 500 Fifth Avenue, New York, NY 10110

For information about special discounts for bulk purchases, please contact W. W. Norton Special Sales at specialsales@wwnorton.com or 800-233-4830

Manufacturing by Lakeside Book Company
Production manager: Katelyn MacKenzie

Library of Congress Cataloging-in-Publication Data

Names: Alcee, Michael, author.
Title: Therapeutic improvisation : how to stop winging it and own it as a therapist / Michael Alcee.
Description: First edition. | New York : W. W. Norton & Company, [2022] | "A Norton professional book." | Includes bibliographical references and index.
Identifiers: LCCN 2021038684 | ISBN 9781324019596 (paperback) | ISBN 9781324019602 (epub)
Subjects: LCSH: Psychotherapy. | Psychotherapist and patient.
Classification: LCC RC475 .A43 2022 | DDC 616.89/14--dc23/eng/20211013
LC record available at https://lccn.loc.gov/2021038684

W. W. Norton & Company, Inc., 500 Fifth Avenue, New York, N.Y. 10110
www.wwnorton.com

W. W. Norton & Company Ltd., 15 Carlisle Street, London W1D 3BS

1 2 3 4 5 6 7 8 9 0

This book is lovingly dedicated to Alicia Malca Alcée and all the other sensitive souls out there who strive to make poetry and music out of the stories we have lived and the wonders they contain.

CONTENTS

ACKNOWLEDGMENTS

I would like to thank my editor at Norton, Deborah Malmud, for having the vision and courage to take on this creative and unconventional project with me and for pushing me to own my writing voice in ways I never imagined possible. I'd also like to specially thank Lou Cozolino for sharing and supporting that vision and Jan Mohlman for planting the seeds of this project with talks I gave to her graduate students at William Paterson University.

I'm so grateful to my most admired colleagues for their wholehearted encouragement of this project from the very start: Irvin Yalom, Philip Bromberg, Donnel Stern, Mary Pipher, Nancy McWilliams, Adam Grant, Daniel Pink, Ellen Langer, Antonio Damasio, Marilyn Charles, Ghislaine Boulanger, James Wilk, Sandra Buechler, Gerald Corey, and Gurmeet Kanwal. I'm also grateful to my special mentors from afar: Daniel J. Siegel, Allan Schore, Iain McGilchrist, Susan Cain, Howard Gardner, Roger Lewin, and Oliver Sacks.

I'd like to thank my mother, Alicia Malca Alcée, for teaching me the joys and beauty of being a therapist–artist; this book is dedicated to your blessed memory.

I'd like to acknowledge my sister Julie Alcée and my uncle

Thomas Lombardi for their continued encouragement on this project ("Bohemian Rhapsody!"), my father, Cyril Alcée, for suspecting that I was a writer from the start, Susan Pogemiller for her ever-artistic inspiration, Kathleen and George Worthington for fostering my love of poetry and the imagination, and my favorite English teacher George Blouin for showing me the life-altering power of literature.

A special thank you goes out to all the members of the Contemporary Poets Society at the Rye Free Reading Room, a group I curated that reawakened my love for poetry and reminded me that art truly heals and connects.

I'm sending out a special thank you to my writing cheerleaders, accountability partners, and discriminating readers Debbie Heiser, Chris Willard, Mitch Abblett, Paula Melo, and the whole community of therapist–writers at *Psychwriters*. A heartfelt thank you to Hilary Jacobs Hendel for being my unexpected and just-at-the-right-time writing mentor who saw my potential and gave so generously of her time and expertise.

A very special thank you to Nathan Eckel who helped launch this book project with our podcast series *Live Life Creatively*. Thank you for riffing with me and making this book a stronger project because of your insights and encouragement.

This book wouldn't be possible without very special musical mentors, Avraham Sternklar and Andy Jaffe, who taught me the beauty and depth of the classical and jazz worlds. Nor would this book be possible without the discriminating and poetic vision of my psychological mentors: Donald Kalsched, Maxson McDowell, Thomas Menaker, Anton Hart, Webb Garrison III, Charles Corliss, and John McCabe.

For learning how to teach psychotherapy, I am indebted to my own special teachers: Laurie Heatherington, Gail Newman, George Goethals, Susan Engel, Frederic Wertz, Dean McKay, Eric Chen, Jeffrey Dyke, and Jeffrey B. Rubin. All of these individuals modeled to me what it means to be a curious, kind, and creative therapist ever ready to be of service.

I'd like to acknowledge with much appreciation the public lecture series at the William Alanson White Institute for being the psychological jazz club where I learned many of the licks found herein.

I'd like to thank my colleagues and students at the Manhattan School of Music for fostering my interests in a musical understanding of the therapeutic process and pushing me to do as many public talks as possible on this subject. Special thanks to Monica Christensen, Shara Sand, Lisa Yui, Stefon Harris, John Pagano, Anne Shikany, and Jim Gandry.

A special thank you goes out to all of the wonderfully creative and talented supervisees who inspired this project and wholeheartedly shared their work and process with me. Ellen Whalen and Jenny Tanis, thank you for the many walking supervisions that brought these pages to life.

This book wouldn't be possible or interesting without the dedicated heart, soul, and music of my most wonderful clients. I am enormously grateful to be able to play on the stage with you in sessions and here again on these pages.

Finally, I'd like to thank my wife, Meryl, and my son, Aidan, for teaching me daily the joys of improvising and tracking what new song we'll be playing together next.

PROLOGUE

If you are anything like I was as a graduate student and early career clinician, you've been trying to put together all that you have learned, in class and in the consulting room, into a coherent voice that is authentically yours. You've been looking for the tools and inspiration to guide you in this crucial metatask that is presumed to just coalesce naturally. Most importantly, you've been searching for a companion along the way to help you find the answers and ask the questions that even veteran therapists don't talk about as much as they really should.

In short, you've been looking for the therapeutic version of that perfect TED talk that can teach you how to start making music out of the noise of therapy.

An artistic and neuroscientific manifesto, this book will provide you with a conceptual and practical framework to define and develop your therapeutic voice, that mysterious yet all-encompassing style that will run like an invisible thread through all of your work as a clinician. Better yet, it will teach you the art of *therapeutic improvisation*—the interplay of using your voice to engage and expand the music in your clients—and illustrate how that makes this challenging work so fulfilling, creative, and transformational. Drawing heavily on examples from literature, music, and movies, this guide will open your eyes to a whole new way of viewing the process of your therapeutic growth and provide you with an inspiring array of clinically artistic moments.

Don't worry if you don't think of yourself as an artist—even, as we'll see, master therapist Irvin Yalom didn't think of himself as one either—these tools are backed up by the latest neuroscientific research on how we use relationships to heal, repair, and expand.

If you're a supervisor to emerging therapists, this book provides a whole new way of looking at the development of your supervisees, serving as a practical manual to support their clinical and personal growth. With an easy-to-apply transtheoretical model and a variety of clinical examples to draw on, your work with supervisees will become even more productive and fulfilling, and together you will reenvision therapy as an artistic process in itself.

This book is grounded in an empirical framework of the most up-to-date neuroscientific research on how the therapeutic process really works in practice, and parallels how 21st-century start-up culture and contemporary neuroscience reimagine and synergize right- and left-brain functioning. Throughout these pages, I show how the art of psychotherapy flows organically from the science of interpersonal neurobiology.

Drawing on empirical research, clinical practice, and inspiration from quotes and TED talks by renowned artists, this book is sure to be appreciated by anybody who wants to develop and celebrate their artistic voice as a therapist in the 21st century.

HOW TO READ
THIS BOOK

I know you're busy and tired. Whether you're working away at your field placement or externship or internship site, jumping through the next hoop of your graduate school program, writing your dissertation, finding your soulmate, or raising a family, you don't have much time.

This book can be read straight through or a chapter at a time. Each chapter will be a free-standing sculpture of inspiration, knowledge, and fun for you to remember again why you came to this field and how you are bringing something special to it too. Did I mention that you are an artist in the making? Yeah, pretty surprising. More on that in the pages to come.

There will be loads of metaphors and images to help you put together difficult concepts. And even better, there will be music, movies, literature, and art so you're thoroughly entertained along the way.

Why all this multidisciplinary fuss and an uber-focus on the humanities? Like our patients, we learn and grow best in an integrated fashion, where the right and left brain are equally respected and shown ways to collaborate again. We are also meant to think and feel our way through stories. As therapists, we all know the tremendous power of witnessing, how it enables us to own, express, and contain our multitudes inside, and even more, how it enables us to help the world itself celebrate the diversity of our unique humanity.

So yeah, this book takes each of you on as my special supervisees from a distance. I'll try to anticipate your hopes, fears, and struggles, and provide guidance and a curated ride so you can feel safe enough to enjoy and free enough to wonder and wander.

Each chapter ends with two exercises that function like lead sheets for musicians, a summary of the essential points of the chapter and takeoff points for practicing and improvising on the tips. The first exercise of each chapter focuses on your role as the therapist–artist and your productions, while the second exercise focuses on your own personal process and is geared toward proper self-care. These are done to provide more integration and interconnection between your artistic and personal creativity.

An appendix at the end includes curated recommendations of diverse TED and TEDx talks that echo the ideas and concepts set forth in each chapter. A short paragraph introduces them and their connection to our work as therapists. Dubbed TED Tie-Ins, these talks serve to inspire and fire up your imagination as artists, innovators, and creators.

Finally, just in case you're more of a visual learner or you appreciate movies like me, there will be a number of film scenes used to illustrate working with clients and delving into the poignant range of this heartbreakingly beautiful condition of being human. If you're a supervisor or professor assigning this book, you can easily find and show scenes from the various films to more deeply engage with the content.

I've written this book in hopes that it will be an "untextbook," showcasing all that you'd hope to get in a comprehensive text with much more fun, practicality, and entertainment. With its personalized approach to helping you find your voice, make music, and improvise on therapy's infinite changes, I also like to think of it as a "meta-how-to" book, one that will provide you with enough of a big-picture sweep and zeroed-in close-ups to help you put the picture together in your own creative and unique way.

Now, go, read a little. And read a little more, and let's start playing so we can make more interesting music together.

FROM WINGING IT TO OWNING IT

In my music, I'm trying to play the truth of what I am. The reason it's difficult is because I'm changing all the time.

—Jazz bassist, composer, and bandleader
Charles Mingus *(in Fawcett, 1978)*

Weaving Through All Sorts of Things

It's not easy to learn the craft of therapy. There's so many of us and so many of them, and we're changing all the time. Whether we subscribe to jazz bassist Charles Mingus's ethos above or muster the courage to confront the changes David Bowie (1971) sings about, it's humbling, confusing, and downright scary to become a therapist. It's certainly not for the faint of heart.

We can take consolation from none other than Fred Rogers, the iconic children's television host and unrecognized champion of psychological improvisation. In the opening scene of the documentary *Won't You Be My Neighbor?*, a young Rogers is tickling the ivories when he beckons us over to muse with him (Neville et al., 2018). Shot in the grainy black-and-white of a 1960s home movie, Rogers, like a new therapist himself, is still finding his voice.

It seems to me there are different themes in life. And one
of my main jobs . . . is to help children through some
of the difficult modulations of life. Because it's easy,
for instance, to go from C to F. But there are so many
modulations that aren't so easy. For instance, to go from
F to F sharp, you've got to weave through all sorts of
things. And it seems to me that if you've got somebody to
help you as you weave . . .

But like so many new therapists, Rogers trails off and doubts
himself. Whereas at first he gazes dreamily into the camera and
is on his way to being enchanted with his own ideas, he quickly
begins to hesitate. As if to say, "What am I talking about? This
is silly!," he shakes his head out of this magical reverie and confesses, "Maybe this is too philosophical. Maybe I'm trying to
combine things that can't be combined, but it makes sense to
me." Ever the artist, the persistent Rogers, who later testifies
in Congress to bring funding back to public television, holds
steady to his belief, even if it isn't fully realized yet. And yes, so
will you soon too.

   This book is a guide to help you make new and unexpected
connections between therapy, music, literature, art, and everything else in the service of becoming better versed in learning
how to read and work with the changes that therapy constantly
throws at us. And this book will help you do this in a way that
is uniquely yours.

   Whether you imagine yourself as a jazz artist being constantly called to take solos on chord changes you are only just
learning or a conductor who is expected to lead without a score,
without even so much as an awareness of what key or tempo
you are really supposed to be in, or you are just newly imagining yourself as an artist on the stage, then you, my friend, are
doing therapy.

It's not for the faint of heart, but once you start getting into it with the help of somebody who can help you weave through "all sorts of things," to borrow Rogers's felicitous phrase, you're in for a lot of fun. And soon enough, it will all make sense to you too.

So Many Changes Coming Your Way

The changes in our patients' emotions, thoughts, and sometimes their very words come at us fast. Like the speed of light—186,000 miles per second if you were curious—these changes are too fast to be fully absorbed and repackaged. A study found these microexpressions only hang out for less than 500 milliseconds (Yan et al., 2013). As new therapists, we feel at the mercy of these changes happening in front of us, as if listening to a song we only wish we had the skills to improvise upon.

I always flash back to John Coltrane's (1976) *Giant Steps.* The first time I heard the 1959 classic, I was mesmerized by Coltrane's capacity to weave in and out of so many changes. The melody itself at the head jauntily jumps around and is inspiring enough, but then when you get to the solos, it's like Coltrane takes a rocket to compete with light itself.

If you haven't heard this tune before, go ahead and find it online or, better yet, get a version where you can see the notes flying by. Don't worry—I'll wait!

Flying at 288 beats per minute, Coltrane gracefully cruises over landscapes far and wide, and as I listen or watch the notes, I imagine the way us therapists just try to keep pace with the many productions of our patients in their subtle shades of sadness, anger, frustration, and longing. How did Coltrane do this? How do we do this?

We're going to sharpen the vocabulary together, practice

our scales, and learn how to make this interesting music too. But first things first: we need to just recognize how much can happen in only a few moments of a session and begin from the premise that what seems like never-ending uncertainty can be the home of infinite possibility too (Schwartz, 2017).

Neuroscience Is Our Artistic Ally

With this book, you're going to learn how to capitalize on the lightning-fast, instinctive, holistic, and creative way the right brain takes in new changes, through what we'll describe in Chapter 1 as *therapeutic presence*. This is the analogue of a good musician's deep listening capacity, really tuning in and absorbing all of the changes, both when you are accompanying, as you take in your patient's stories, or when you are soloing, helping them to reimagine new possibilities within those stories (Knoblauch, 2000). As you progress, the improvisation will go back and forth such that riffing together, alongside our clients, we become newly enchanted at the many interesting takes we get on what seems like just a simple tune.

There's an iconic Don Hunstein (2017) photograph with John Coltrane in the foreground, deep in reflection like Rodin's *The Thinker*, with a blurred Miles Davis playing trumpet in the background for the epic 1959 album *Kind of Blue*. Made into a meme, it reads, "There's listening, and then there's *listening . . .* " That's the kind of profound tuning and connection that we're going to cultivate together, and it sets the stage for the great fun that is the mutual improvisation of therapy.

As we get the right brain tuned and fit, then we'll progress to sharing it with the left brain's marvelous capacity to put precise and specific verbal form—language itself—to the many interesting and essential changes that your patient is trying to convey, the feelings and thoughts they are desperately wishing to express with your help. The left brain will come online in the form of *therapeutic authority*, and it will be focused, selective, and impactful, providing your patient with something actionable and transformative to reshape their understanding, feelings, and behavior. This is where the mutual improvisations begin to really take flight.

You'll be able to own it in the moment—not after 10 or 20 sessions—because as you get used to this kind of skill, like music, you just can't separate listening from playing and playing from listening. They will feed each other, and you will toggle back and forth to make something greater than the sum of its parts, and surprise each other with how enjoyable and effective it truly is. Who knew making art—the therapeutic process itself—could be this powerful? As one client told me one while leaving the office, "If I had known therapy was going to be this fun and helpful, I would have done it years ago!"

By putting these skills together, you'll have a distinctive, flexible, and solid *therapeutic voice*—like an artist's voice—which will allow you to be highly responsive to your patients and, just as important, responsive to the constantly changing music within you. When we get these two capacities put in place, just like the right and left brain themselves or like AC/DC current, we'll have you operating in a whole different sphere. You'll be amazed at how what used to feel like just winging it has now become owning it.

But like most of us starting out, let's begin with our nightmare scenarios, when the changes are coming at us way too fast and we feel like we are flying blind and about to crash.

Winging It and Flying Blind

Writing is like driving at night in the fog.
You can only see as far as your headlights, but
you can make the whole trip that way.

—E. L. Doctorow

It's so difficult in the moment to figure out what to do and say to make our clients, especially our most difficult ones, feel better and open for creative growth. And many times, this is because we're actually improvising unconsciously, flying blind into only hazily known territory. It's the fog Doctorow references in the art of writing, except that therapy has even higher stakes. We are flying in an airplane or helicopter. So many controls to master, and pretty frightening up at that altitude!

Let's start with a true nightmare scenario. Imagine you are the therapist, and a 20-something comes into your office. You know he has a brilliant and sharp mind and that he works as a janitor. He sits on your chair and sighs good-naturedly, "All right, let's do it. I'm pumped. Let's let the healing begin."

Soon enough, as you begin to ask him questions about his life and his interests, he's off to the races, commenting glibly on your décor, asking where you got your books, saying you've got the wrong books. As quickly as that starts, a new pissing contest emerges, with you and him competing about how much you each bench press, and then he walks over to a painting you've made, critiques it, and says you are one step away from cutting off your ear.

Noticing your fraying patience, he diagnoses you as on the edge and then hits you in the jugular by claiming you've married the wrong woman. "What, did she have an affair or something?" he taunts.

Remember Coltrane's Giant Steps? In a matter of seconds,

you've moved from civility to savagery, and at the end of this scene, the first meeting between Will and Sean in the movie *Good Will Hunting* (Van Sant, 1997), Sean grabs Will by the neck and cadences the session with: "If you ever disrespect my wife again, I will end you. I will fucking end you. . . . Got that, chief?" When the changes come at you this fast, it's no wonder you want to hide behind your techniques and the role of expert. Who wants to be in the line of this emotional fire? Sometimes it might make you wonder, who would undertake this job willingly?

Relational psychoanalyst Philip Bromberg (2011) reminds us that when we tap into areas of dissociated trauma like Will's, a tsunami of affect overtakes both therapist and patient. And what could become a space of creativity instead become lacunae of anguish, despair, and aggression.

In Chapters 1 and 2, we'll talk in depth about how and why this happens, providing useful terminology that will function as leverage for your creative therapeutic work. These concepts— multiplicity, enactment, and not-me, to name just a few—will provide the scales and arpeggios you need to master the difficult passages that so often occur with patients like Will. For now, note that Bromberg (2006) tells us that what we need to do with patients like this is to help awaken the dreamer and begin the process of creating a small space of reflective and emotional curiosity.

When we get to this place, we get to the exciting part that moves beyond winging it. When we can track the changes, and understand and see why things are devolving—after the fact and with practice, even in the moment—we take an explosive situation and harness the nuclear energy to light up a city and do some phenomenal creative work with our patients.

What does this look like? Let's take another nightmare scenario and see how it can turn into a dream.

The Moments We Dream About:
Opening Up Creative Space

I dwell in Possibility—A fairer House than Prose.

—Emily Dickinson

Having taken a vow of silence against his dysfunctional family—a silent protest and act of rebellion—Dwayne is a 15-year-old setting his sights on becoming an Air Force pilot. It is his unconscious way of transcending the problems and despair of his family life and a lifelong dream. But today, while passing time in the family VW Bug on a cross-country trip, his 7-year-old sister is playfully goading him to tell her what colors he sees in a picture after confirming he has 20/20 vision. And he can't make it out. He gets the colors all wrong.

His suicidal gay uncle, just out from being institutionalized, no stranger himself to existential crisis, is the one to calmly break the news. Shocked to find that he is color-blind, it quickly dawns on Dwayne that his lifelong dream is in jeopardy. Pounding on the doors of the car in motion, he is set to explode, and as the family abruptly pulls over the car, Dwayne runs down a ditch on the side of the road and howls the longest and most plaintive "fuck!" his family has ever heard.

The whole family knows the reality. Dwayne can't be an Air Force pilot, but they don't know what to do. The changes have come on so fast and furious that everybody struggles to help him. And what's worse, the family is already in a rush to fulfill younger daughter Olive's dream of participating in the Little Miss Sunshine pageant.

Mom goes first. Distraught, neurotically struggling to calm him yet unable to keep her own anxiety in check, it completely backfires. She tries to get him to remember that they are all family, but Dwayne doesn't want to hear it. He is tired of the family's collection of deficiencies and finally unleashes what he has been holding in for so long: "I hate you! Divorce. Bankrupt. Suicide. You're losers."

Dad is up next, but he's too concerned with the time, considering leaving someone with Dwayne so they can get to their destination more quickly. And then up comes little sister Olive, sauntering down the hill awkwardly in her oversized red cowboy boots.

Like a good therapist, she approaches gingerly, gives him a knowing look of concern, and then sits right next to him as she puts her arm around him and leans her head on his shoulder. A nonverbal tour de force, she shows him how much she is hurting with him and how much she cares, and in her innocent gesture, he begins to heal.

As we watch this scene from the movie *Little Miss Sunshine* (Faris & Dayton, 2006), we get a reminder of how we are all winging it when it comes to the everyday upheavals of life and how especially hard it is when our deepest fears and dreams are placed starkly before us.

If we can imagine ourselves as this little girl for a moment, we can see how learning how to improvise can truly serve us, how we can take in the right-brain-to-right-brain communication of an emotional storm and ground it in an intentional and mindful act of compassion (Siegel & Bryson, 2012; Siegel, 2010; Schore, 2019). Keep in mind that we can learn a lot from a child: they are right-brain dominant from about age 1 to 3 years, and the left brain comes fully online by age 7. Ironically, they are our greatest teachers for how to reintegrate our right brain into our work as therapists.

The movement from winging it to owning it comes in the special improvisation that allows a creative space to open up. This is the possibility that Emily Dickinson refers to as the fairer house of poetry. Improvisation, like good poetry, works on the turn, the pivot that moves something away from seeming chaos and into a surprisingly interesting new place.

In his TED talk "Lead Like the Great Conductors," Israeli conductor Itay Talgam (2009) talks about the importance of being in control and yet creating an opening, qualities we'll need in full to master this art of therapeutic improvisation. Showcasing Carlos Kleiber's conducting of a dynamic Beethoven symphony, Talgam says:

> He is not telling them what to do. When he does this [gestures hands wildly like a baton coming down], it's not, "Take your Stradivarius and like Jimi Hendrix smash it on the floor." He says, "This is a gesture of the music. I'm opening up space for you to put in another layer of interpretation, that is, another story."

Learning From Improv Comedy: Accepting the Offer

How do we open up this space in therapy? We can learn a lot from the arts. In improv comedy, the cardinal rule is to say "Yes, and" to accept the offer of whatever is given and to use it as a springboard for new material to emerge collaboratively.

In *Little Miss Sunshine*, Olive's character is the only one who wholeheartedly embraces Dwayne's offer of despair, sadness, and fear. Instead of countering his emotional experience with, "No, but we really need to get going," or "No, but even though you can't be an Air Force pilot, there are still so many places you can go!" or any other such hollow rejoinder, she stays right with his authentic and alive experience. She goes into the depth of his pain with great courage and is rewarded with his lifting her up as they make their way back up to solid ground together, as the sign "United We Stand" flashes symbolically at the close of the scene.

Contrast this with Will and Sean in *Good Will Hunting*. Ironically, Robin Williams (Sean), ever the improv genius, can't help himself as an actor, giving, accepting, and extending the offers given by acting partner Matt Damon (Will). A classic Williams comedic improv moment textures the unfolding drama between the sparring pair:

> **WILLIAMS:** You know you'd be better off shoving that cigarette up your ass? It'd probably be healthier for you.
>
> **DAMON:** Yeah, I know. It really gets in the way of my yoga.
>
> **WILLIAMS:** You work out, huh?

But as a character, Will does everything in his power to block and cancel any of Sean's bids for closeness and connection. He subverts him at every pass and, like a chess master, finds a way of turning Will's offers of affection into a quick succession of checkmates.

In both movie examples, you can see how quickly the weather can intensify or clear up, and how challenging and rewarding it is to be subjected to it as a helper. In Chapters 2 and 3, we're going to define and label the neuroscientific underpinnings of these experiences so that you are better armed with the science that happens behind the scenes in the making of the art that is therapy, the intentional practice of learning how to weather, navigate, and chart your way through these inevitable storms.

To borrow from award-winning educators and clinical professors Dan Siegel and Tina Payne Bryson (2012), we'll have a model to "stay on the river of well-being" as therapists and find balance between the "banks of chaos and rigidity."

What Is Therapeutic Improvisation?

Improvisation: to compose or utter without
preparation, borrowed from the Latin
improvisus, *meaning not seen before.*

Therapeutic improvisation, like jazz or comedy improvisation, is a paradoxical enterprise of prepared spontaneity and disciplined freedom. We are loose and free enough to let our minds and hearts wander and deliberate and disciplined enough to stay right on track. And when we unite and integrate these dual functions, new, productive, and interesting things happen.

New emotional experiences, like new harmonic colors and unexpected cadences, are brought into the music by our clients and ourselves. We feel things that were there but not spoken about, we sense into layers of emotional history of the many songs that were played before the one we are working on currently, and they help us carry the tune even better together. Novel cognitive perspectives enable us to see the fuller contexts of theirs and our inner architectures and free us up to vary it for new approaches toward rebuilding, renovating, and reshaping a landscape we once thought was static.

In short, therapeutic improvisation allows us to play with possibilities within the grounded structures and vocabulary of the music of the psyche. And as we'll see in Chapter 2, this requires a solid understanding of interpersonal neurobiology, how we are built and function from the inside out and how relationships enhance, support, or inhibit these creative possibilities.

Therapeutic improvisation allows us to enter into the highly technical and nuanced world of ever-changing and dynamic harmonic moments, to study their complex architecture in myriad diagnostic forms and possibilities (McWilliams, 1999), and yet also brings us into the nonlinear emotional experience that emerges largely unbidden moment by moment (Stern, 2017). It is at once formulated and unformulated (Stern, 2009), with its creative possibilities occurring, as Freud originally showed us in his earliest writings on Fraulein Elisabeth Von R., in the spaces and gaps:

> I would begin by getting the patient to tell me what was known to her and I would carefully note the points at which some train of thought remained obscure or some link in the causal chain seemed to be missing. (Breuer & Freud, 1995, p. 139)

Like a good neurologist and artist—while never winning the coveted Nobel Prize, he won the Goethe Prize in literary achievement—Freud recognized that much more was happening in those synaptic spaces, and it was our creative work to help our clients become freer, braver, and bolder in relationship to them. Intuitively, he recognized the power of the therapeutic relationship itself to facilitate that process, borrowing the therapist's trust, courage, curiosity, and resourcefulness to open up a reliable process within oneself to learn how to improvise and free associate again. Revolutionary and prescient, Freud foresaw the funny way we humans are built to integrate our primal right-brain emotions—what he termed *primary process*—with our more dominant and socialized left-brain reason and civility.

As Jungian analyst Donald Kalsched (2013) points out, echoing Winnicott's (2016) notion of potential space, the creative moment occurs at the space between Adam's finger and the finger of God in Michelangelo's great rendering in the Sistine Chapel. This is also the home of jazz, which you can hear in the pregnant pauses and rests of a Miles Davis solo in the epic album *Kind of Blue* (1959). The creative space opens up, as we showed earlier in the chapter, as if out of a dream. Therapeutic improvisation, to borrow from psychoanalyst Thomas Ogden (1997), is a wakeful form of dreaming, one that allows us to create and inhabit more space simultaneously and, in so doing, to transcend both.

The point of therapeutic improvisation, like jazz improvisation, is to recognize and unearth old forms and create new ones through the special vehicle that is the relationship itself. We trade solos back and forth—what jazz musicians call trading fours— and improvise together in relational therapy, become equal partners in learning how to read our own changes and listen deeply to each other, transforming our individual stories into creative works of art.

Therapy's Changes: Playing the Blues

The space between the idea of something and its
reality is always wide and deep and dark.
—Jamaica Kincaid (1991)

Every patient comes into psychotherapy to play the blues, some variety of suffering that they are bringing to us for our attention and care. Whether a 12-, 16-, or 32-bar version or a round of multiple choruses, it's so often the melancholy found in that crushed blue note that inspires us to seek a therapist to help read the changes: why can't I stop feeling this anxiety, depression, social disconnection, or some other form of human unhappiness?

Unbeknownst to himself, Freud ushered in psychotherapy as an improvisatory art form. From his earliest work with Miss

Lucy R. and Fraulein Elisabeth Von R. in *Studies on Hysteria* (Breuer & Freud, 2000), where he guided patients to "concentrate" and yet openly report "faithfully whatever appeared before [their] inner eye or passed through [thei]r memory at the moment" (Breuer & Freud, 1995, p. 145), to his primary advice to beginning therapists on evenly hovering attention (Freud & Gay, 1995), Freud championed both free association and a disciplined approach to following the dynamic changes of the psyche.

His method required and celebrated a spontaneous and improvisational receptivity to experience. In allowing patients the freedom not to worry about censoring any of their thoughts and feelings, he echoed jazz vibraphonist Stefon Harris's (2011) keen observation: "There are no mistakes on the bandstand!"

According to Harris (2011), one shouldn't force or commandeer the band but rather open and flow into new territory together, with both the ensemble and soloist truly listening and expressing simultaneously. With the complementary processes of evenly hovering attention and free association, Freud's work mirrored the jazz aesthetic. His was a revolutionary movement toward mutual interplay and, to bend Sullivan's (1954) phrase, profoundly observant participation.

Therapeutic Improvisation Realized: A Case Illustration

"How is it that we always discover new things when we are talking together?"

I was talking to a jazz pianist who was struggling with performance anxiety at gigs—freezing up internally when it was time for her to solo—and confused in her relationships, where she emotionally took a backseat yet secretly yearned to be more in the spotlight.

"I don't know. Maybe it's because we find something and fill in the spaces together. It's funny how it just seems to make its way into our field of vision, isn't it? It's like we have this great melody that we keep reharmonizing."

We had been talking, like many of my conservatory students, about the paradoxical benefits and costs of Olympic-level training, of the expansive straitjacket that is becoming an expert in a specialty craft. We were riffing together on how being in the role is a mixed blessing, how it's not always so easy to be the golden child of the family.

She confided in me that being in the position of soloing, and possibly taking away the focus from others, produced anxiety. After all, she knew how competitive this field was, and it just felt cruel to be hogging so much. It wasn't easy being this chosen one. As in the biblical story of Joseph, she wondered if people would resent her if she shone too brightly, that maybe they would want to unseat her, that she would lose her balance and fall. Or, like Joseph, she mused, would she be thrown into a pit?

"It's like you're only standing on one foot. And that foot is your expertise, and if you don't hold it up, you will inevitably fall and fall far." An image of Icarus's wings melting flashed through my mind. I didn't realize it at the time, but my right brain was beginning to riff on a subversive view of Icarus borrowed from Jack Gilbert's (2005) poem "Failing and Falling."

"Well, I was one of the few pianists chosen for this program, and I don't want all the other pianists who didn't make it to feel like they were beaten by this impostor. It's my job to really show them that I belong here."

"It's like you don't have room to slip, that you're not allowed to be honest with the fact that being so successful also sucks!"

Her eyes widened with what appeared to be the beginning of a mischievous grin.

"Yes, I said it—it sucks." We both laughed. "I think the other foot that you're not allowed to put on the ground is the one that is free to fail and fall" (Gilbert, 2005). "Without it, though, it's no wonder you feel so wobbly at times."

Like a dream, her golden child image kept stirring in me. It was like a riff I knew wanted to be brought back into the music. Internally, I remembered some of the harmonic changes from her family story, how she had been expected to make up for a brother who fell into drugs and a father who had left the scene because of his own addiction problem. She was holding something very important up—the mantle of success and possibility—and up until this point, we had not yet found the form for it.

My mind wandered to a picture of the squeaky clean *American Idol* host and TV/radio personality Ryan Seacrest. I imagined him doing something scandalous, petty, and mean, and the troll-like backlash that would inevitably crash against this polished and wholesome spokesman. I shared that I thought it would be great if he did something like this, that he deserved it!

There was a tentative delight in this. To be the devil so willingly seemed to create a whole new set of harmonic changes to incorporate. It was like we put in some tritone substitutions and chromatic turnarounds to take one of those stately ballads and make it dissonant and edgy.

She connected this to the feeling she sometimes had in her relationship. She felt like she so often had to play the role of the good girlfriend, the caring and thoughtful one who, as with her brother, had to be ever ready for something awful to happen.

My mind wandered again to another work of art: Oscar Wilde's *An Ideal Husband* (Wilde, 2017). How difficult and challenging it is to be an ideal husband because of the ways in which, inevitably, there will be so little room for error. We began to riff on how being an ideal girlfriend made it difficult for her to try out any other possible roles, or have the freedom to be too self-interested and more assertive.

I began to hear Sarah Vaughan's version of "The Nearness of You" playing in my head (Vaughan et al., 2000). I shared with her this lovely moment in the tune where she completely reharmonizes the lyric "When you're in my arms and I feel you so close to me, all my wildest dreams come true" with chromatic substitutions. What is at once an open longing also becomes a melancholy haunting, a complicated ache. We began to note the possibility of moving outside the stereotyped romantic ballad where the difficulties of losing oneself in a relationship can simultaneously coexist with the desire to feel that dream of love.

She started to think about her boyfriend, and how at times he wouldn't really take in her interests or her needs and instead would use them as a springboard to talk about his own. It reminded her of the jazz concept of superimposition, when one plays a whole different set of chord changes over those already in use. When done right and with a rhythm section that is really tracking the shift, superimposition can sound really hip and interesting, like McCoy Tyner's solo on "Bessie's Blues" (Coltrane, 1964). In that tune, he jumps out of the regular blues chord changes and soars into wholly new keys, making us feel as if we are temporarily launching into space and coming back down to Earth.

Unfortunately, my patient sighed, when a player is just trying to sound cool and think about themselves, it all falls apart. She began to see that when her boyfriend's narcissistic needs took over the music, they weren't truly playing together. Moreover, she began to notice how this played out both in her relationships and in her family, and how we were both recognizing and reconfiguring old forms into new possibilities. It was no wonder that we were discovering so much in each session together.

Bringing It All Together

Relational therapy, as Freud truly intended it, is a jazz art form. It makes room for us to be the trickster, like Thelonius Monk playing with syncopated dissonances, the pensive Bill Evans with his lush and sophisticated voicings, the manic Charlie Parker frantically moving in and out of his bop solos, or the soulful, otherworldly John Coltrane aching with love.

It is the art that celebrates the multiplicity of self and provides a master class in learning the infinite variety of chord changes that constitute it. For as we see above, within each self-state is a different set of possible chord changes to know, share, and enjoy, and this happens best in the mutual improvisational interplay that Freud began.

Relational therapy enables the patient to be both the bandleader, like Ellington quarterbacking the group, and the virtuoso, dropping right in as the soloist (Hasse, 1995). To riff on Harry Stack Sullivan (1954), therapy's main task is to reconnect the benevolent witness and the active participant, allowing us to be both subject and object in flexible and creative ways. As Freud had it, psychotherapy expands our capacity to be free to love and work, to make new and original forms out of what is in our past and present, and, in so doing, to be able to open up to the uncharted territory both within and before us in the improvisational moment that becomes our future.

The Humble Beginnings of Relational Improvisation

All children are born artists, the problem is
to remain an artist as we grow up.

—Pablo Picasso

We do know that no one gets wise enough
to really understand the heart of another,
though it is the task of our life to try.

—Louise Erdrich

We start out curious and improvisatory about everything. Children ask questions to learn how and why things and people work the way they do and what new ways you can imagine them otherwise. In her fascinating book *The Hungry Mind: The Origins of Curiosity in Childhood*, developmental psychologist Susan Engel (2015) sheds light on how curiosity and creativity both develop and diminish. In a study of 3- and 4-year-olds, Tizard and Hughes (1984) found that children asked an average of 26 questions per hour at home with their mothers, 60% of which were aimed at learning something new.

But something shifts at school. In the place where education is supposed to thrive, the same children asked only two questions per hour. Lindfors (1987) found that less than a third of kindergarteners' questions were expressions of curiosity. Engel's own research confirmed this. She found 2.36 episodes of curiosity in a two-hour period for kindergarteners and only 0.48 in a classroom of fifth graders.

Anecdotal evidence brings home the point. Daniel Pink (2006) notes how the Hallmark creative wizard Gordon MacKenzie surveyed how many students were artists in the classes he visited. Every student in kindergarten and first grade catapulted their hands into the air, three-fourths in second grade, only a few children in third grade, and by sixth grade, not a single, solitary hand went up.

Like the main character in *The Little Prince*, we all start out as creative and curious artists, all of us flexible little improvisers. A little boy delightedly creates a drawing of a boa constrictor swallowing an elephant, expecting his audience to be both frightened and wowed. So proud of the inner world he is mastering and making, he is disillusioned to find that adults, the arbiters of the external social world, only see a hat. Crestfallen, he concludes, "Grown-ups never understand anything by themselves, and it is tiresome for children to be always and forever explaining things to them."

Children are also masters of improvisation and spontaneity. After writing the words for this chapter waiting to gain access to our bedroom after finishing my morning shower, my 2-year-old son wouldn't let me pass unless I played an impromptu game. "Delivery!" he cried. And I had to open the door, hold out my hands, and say, "What's this??" A letter instantly appeared—his improvisation—and I began to read it intently as he whimsically closed the door. Like the famous squiggle games of pediatrician and child analyst Donald Winnicott, it was now my turn to deliver. I brought him a puzzle and then later a pizza, both of which he incorporated into his own next delivery. We two began to improvise there—me in my towel, him in his pajamas— playing the funny game we all play of negotiating reality and imagination for the upcoming day.

These improvisation games, though made of magic, are not without their hiccups. There are times when it is easy and intuitive to weave in the red string that my son calls "Bonnie the Doggie" into a conversation and other times when something goes terribly wrong and I miss a beat. One day we were delightfully throwing a ball and then searching together for it like detectives in each of the rooms of our house. When my son threw the ball, instinctively and proudly I caught it. He started to wail, "No, Dada, no!"

Quickly I had to read and understand the changes in his face and sequence back and understand the game I was really playing. In the moment, though, I felt like a terrible father, an utter failure, and said with the easy inclination to strike back in my own twisted pride, "But I caught the ball! Isn't that what I'm supposed to do?"

With a moment of quick reflection, I realized I had missed the point. I said, "Buddy, did you not want Dada to catch the ball?," to which he nodded eagerly. "Shall we try again and look for the ball together in the room now?"

Instantly, the storm clouds began to dissipate, and we were both back to our more typical sunny weather together. Without hesitation, we both skipped toward the rooms to find the ball, and I learned an important lesson: in order to be right, we have to be very wrong much of the time, and have the courage and humility to stay through to understand the subtle process happening silently underfoot.

The Detrimental Effects of Losing Improvisational Curiosity

As Picasso and de Saint-Exupéry warn, the curiosity and spontaneity we find naturally in children quickly fades, and this is terribly detrimental to our individual and collective well-being. Psychoanalyst Anton Hart highlights the need for therapists to cultivate curiosity in themselves and their patients. He views lack of curiosity as central not only to individual psychopathology but also to the collective ills of prejudice, discrimination, and othering. Rather than focus merely on cultural competence, he rightfully recommends addressing diversity through a curiosity and openness that safeguards against the automatic ways we can all marginalize and stereotype.

In one of the top 10 most-viewed TED talks of all time,

novelist Chimamanda Ngozi Adichie (2009) echoes this sentiment. Speaking on the danger of a single story, Adichie noted how difficult it was to see herself in the British and American literature she read as a child because it didn't include her. She speaks of the humorous and dangerous ways her American classmates limited her as a Nigerian woman, surprised at her fluency in English and that her "tribal music" was Mariah Carey: "My roommate had a single story of Africa: a single story of catastrophe. In this single story, there was no possibility of Africans being similar to her in any way, no possibility of feelings more complex than pity, no possibility of a connection as human equals." Adichie indicts herself, noting the ease with which she herself could miss the other stories of her poor houseboy Fide, not seeing his family's capacity for other kinds of wealth and respect. She also confesses her shame at reducing the story of Mexicans to the single story of the abject immigrant so common in the American media.

But Adichie insists on the power of curiosity and empathy— the magical ingredients we possess in abundance in childhood— to redress this and save us all from the one story that becomes the only story. We are all guilty and susceptible, she says, to that single story, and it flattens our experience and overlooks the many stories that form us. However, echoing Alice Walker, she reminds us that by rejecting this and realizing that there is never any single story about any place, we regain paradise.

Paradise Regained: Uniting Child's Mind and Expert's Mind

Children provide a master class in the call-and-response improvisation that invites everyone into the game, and they also show all the signs of a developing capacity to showcase their own individual artistic vision too. Playing in the basement later in

the day, my son rides his tricycle from store to store. When I
park in the wrong spot, he tells me, "No, Dada, that is inside
the house. This is outside!" Here we have the forerunner of the
yin and yang of an artistic and therapeutic voice: the capacity
to be receptive and open on the one hand—child's mind—and
discriminating and confident on the other.

The beginner's or child's mind is essential for us to be effective as therapist–artists, but it isn't enough. We also need the
counterbalance of what I term *expert's mind*, the discriminating
and confident approach of the best of the adult world: know-
how and experience. Not coincidentally, the jazz musician is the
perfect embodiment of this marriage.

Expanding Your Range
and Holding Court

So why is this so important for you as a new therapist? It's all
in the service of expanding your repertoire and your range. But
remember, there's an implicit bias in our education system and
even in our parenting that tells us that in order to be a true
expert at something, we have to be practicing from when we are
just out of the womb.

In the book *Range: Why Generalists Triumph in a Specialized
World*, sports writer David Epstein (2019) writes of a 7-month-
old bringing a putter along with him in his walker and at age
2 amazing Bob Hope on national television with the crack of a
drive whizzing by his astonished face. We are quickly and easily impressed by a Tiger Woods, but it is very easy to forget the
Rogers—like tennis great Roger Federer—who try out a whole
bunch of skills and then later focus them into their chosen craft.

I only half-jokingly tell my patients—especially the conservatory folks—and my supervisees that my goal for them is to
help them expand their range, like Meryl Streep does in each

role she plays. It is this capacity to profoundly empathize with those around you—to tune in to others' deepest hopes and fears—and simultaneously stay connected to their own that is your human birthright and our greatest superpower.

An empathic depth perception is one of the powers that actress Meryl Streep uses to inhabit her myriad iconic roles, from *Sophie's Choice* to *Doubt* to *The Devil Wears Prada*. And it is also highlighted in the impassioned and personal way she speaks of humanity's greatest gift: "Why and how did we evolve with this weak and useless passion intact within the deep heart's core? And the answer as I've formulated it to myself is that empathy is the engine that powers all the best in us."

A class act on and off the court, Roger Federer also provides a unique lesson for aspiring therapists: the importance of cultivating the personal evenly alongside the professional. Like Fred Rogers, it is not really a persona we use in order to become effective therapists, it is an intentional melding of the artist within and the artist without that becomes such an inviting, warm, and intriguing presence that allows our patients to join in the fun of the serious art that is psychotherapy.

Tapping Into the Force: You Must Unlearn What You Have Learned

This all sounds exciting, but if you're like most new therapists, it's also a little overwhelming. There seems to be so much to put together. It reminds me of how Luke Skywalker in the movie *The Empire Strikes Back* feels when Yoda is first teaching him how to use the Force to levitate his sunken spacecraft (Kershner & Lucas, 1980). Yoda seems so wise, chill, and confident. Even his words, in their poetic and telegraphic syntax, say more with less.

And what a great paradox "the Force" is, because you really

can't force it in order to tap into it. This is what makes it so maddening and yet so profound—we need to surrender ourselves to something bigger temporarily in order to manifest this powerful strength as an individual. It is the great paradox of the artist—to have an individual voice and yet to speak from and to the collective, and somehow carry both.

It's no wonder Luke gets so frustrated when he can't immediately access it and lift his spacecraft out of the mud. He feels so small, hopeless, and ineffectual. Even after hearing Yoda's soliloquy on the interconnectedness of the universe, Luke needs to see it first before he can believe the Force even exists.

Leadership and mentoring expert Ruth Gotian (R. Gotian, personal communication, January 21, 2021) notes that what is really funny about high achievers—Nobel Prize, Tony Award, and Olympic medal winners—is how none of them think of themselves as truly special or high achieving. In fact, only one of the many she has interviewed had their actual medal framed, while virtually all the others had it in a brown paper bag in their underwear drawer, in a safe locked away, or had given it away.

If right now you are a little neurotic and lacking in confidence, like I was as a new therapist, take heart. As an undergrad, I played piano in a jazz ensemble and was wound so tightly that even when the band director cheered on my playing, I'd nearly jump six feet in the air out of fear and tension.

I was so in awe of my jazz piano teacher's instant capacity to play and read changes, how he could listen and in a flash reproduce the exact chords and voicings he had just heard on a recording and make interesting licks out of them. It all went so fast. I tape recorded all my lessons and played them back over and over again just to get a moment's worth of fluency in my practicing.

One afternoon as I was waiting outside for my weekly lesson, I heard my teacher, Andy Jaffe, noodling around between students, playing an amazing bebop-style solo over changes and licks that I only dreamed of playing myself. It was like watching the intricate gears of an exquisite and expensive Swiss watch moving effortlessly around a theme and making time both move and stand still. Nervously, I said, "Hey Andy, aren't you going to write that beautiful lick down?"

"Nah," he said. "If I forget that line, I'm sure another one will come right along."

Even though you might be feeling like a younger version of me right now, I know you'll be feeling like Andy—and now me!—soon enough.

So don't worry about the feeling that you're just winging it right now. Soon enough, you'll be improvising too. Ready to start playing?

Exercises for Introduction

EXERCISE 1: EMBRACING THE CHANGES: FREE-WHEELING CASE NOTES

Express everything you like. No word can hurt you.
None. No idea can hurt you. Not being able to express
an idea or word will hurt you more. Like a bullet.

—Jamaica Kincaid

The only people for me are the mad ones, the ones who
are mad to live, mad to talk, mad to be saved, desirous
of everything at the same time, the ones who never
yawn or say a commonplace thing, but burn, burn,
burn like fabulous yellow roman candles exploding like
spiders across the stars and in the middle you see the
blue centerlight pop and everybody goes "Awww!"

—Jack Kerouac, *On the Road*

In this exercise, we are going to use free-writing as a technique to write daily case notes that bring out the improvisatory side waiting to be integrated into your work as a clinician. We're going to turn case notes on their head, and write them for ourselves instead of the formal ones we write for our records. Instead of worrying about diagnosis and documentation, we're going to take a free-wheeling right-brain approach to case notes similar to Julia Cameron's method in *The Artist's Way* (1992).

When I started doing this as a graduate student, I had an old marble notebook, and I would write away on the train as I came home from my sessions. Sometimes, I would write in between sessions on the computer, fast like the pianist I am, and plunk out all of the different mixed up thoughts and feelings I had about my sessions. I found it a fantastic way to cleanse the palate between sessions and to keep more aligned with myself so I didn't get lost in all of my client's stories and lose track of my own.

If you'd like to think of yourself as an artist, conjure an encouraging image of Jamaica Kincaide or Jack Kerouac with his pages taped together in a scroll so he could continuously plunk out the pages of *On the Road*, Allen Ginsberg taking all the best bits to collage his famous poem "Howl," or confessional poet Anne Sexton being urged by her psychoanalyst to write out her demons.

Don't worry about grammar, or punctuation, and definitely not about any documentation requirements. This is just you, your patient, and your process. Your goal is just to free associate and write about your experience of your sessions today.

Allow your inner child, your trickster, and your rebel to come up in the new things you are seeing and hearing in your sessions with your patient, in yourself, and in the spaces between you. And just write without worrying, stopping, or censoring.

What intrigues you most about today's session? What vexes you? What still confuses you in your client, in yourself, or in the space between you? Give yourself permission to just write about it all with as much curiosity as you can muster, and then keep going until you hit a detour and the critic starts coming up.

Notice the inner critic trying to inhibit and deter you, saying that these notes themselves are silly, that this isn't really serious work and you are wasting your and your patient's time. Why don't you already have this mastered? Shouldn't you be the one who knows already?

Write whatever the critic is saying to or through you and begin to notice how it attempts to sow doubt, confusion, and fear in you. Type it out: "I don't really know what I'm doing and this is stupid. Who am I to think I can help ['insert patient name here'] since I haven't figured out this issue yet myself?" Whatever the doubts are, give them a space to be entertained.

Personify this critic. Does it remind you of an internet troll, a drill sergeant, a football coach, or a stage mom? Does it remind you of any prior critics in your past? Family? Teachers? Classmates? See if you can write about them and how they had—or still have—a hold on you.

We need to get to know this critic well because it is the greatest adversary of our inner Muse, the fountain of inspiration that we need to be in touch with to play and improvise. However, the good news is, once we understand and consciously integrate the critic, it can become the Muse's greatest ally. Discriminating, penetrating, and wise, it will add depth and nuance to your thoughts and feelings, but now it is savage. The critic must be tamed and domesticated for it to be of service.

Notice its savagery, as in meditation when we notice our monkey-mind thoughts attacking us. Is the critic trying to insult, demean, or attack me? I see you, critic, and I choose to come back to my breath. Remember, after all, the word breath comes from the Hebrew word for spirit. We need that spirit to tap into the creativity needed to embrace the changes and learn how to improvise.

For most of us, the personal and the professional are interconnected. Write about your own day, how it felt running late for that meeting or having to finish that paper last night, or how confusing it's been to find your soulmate, but yes, mix it all together. Notice and embrace all the changes, and see how they can all begin dialoguing together even though it just feels like noise.

EXERCISE 2: CONNECTING TO YOUR ARTISTIC LIFE

Remember that pianist who said that if he did not practice
every day he would know, if he did not practice for two
days, the critics would know, after three days, his audiences
would know. A variation of this is true for writers. . . .
The world would catch up with and try to sicken you. If
you did not write every day, the poisons would accumulate
and you would begin to die, or act crazy, or both.

—Ray Bradbury, *Zen in the Art of Writing*

Now it's time just for you. What are the activities, hobbies, tasks, and interests in which you lose time and become totally immersed and engrossed? Where is it, in other words, that you have regular contact with your artistic sides and the Muse? P. S., it doesn't have to just happen only in sessions!

What do you notice about how you feel about minor or major things changing in this activity? For example, if it is a sport, do you notice that having a tennis ball hit to different sides of the court, or by the net or by the baseline intrigues you more and makes you feel challenged? Do you see this more as possibility rather than as uncertainty? If it is sketching or noodling on an instrument, do you notice the ways in which you get excited about partly knowing where you are going but also being surprised by what comes next?

When the critic comes up, as it so often does, what does it say to you? Is this critic a composite of different real figures, or is it an impersonal abstraction that is hard to see? If it is impersonal, can you give it some form with what or who it reminds you of?

Are there reasons this critic needed to protect you from shame, humiliation, or pain? If so, let's give him or her credit and ask him kindly about the fuller story, so we can help the critic begin to work with the Muse.

When you have finished exploring your own artistic life today, see if you can enjoy something artistic outside of yourself. Is it a piece of music, a photograph or painting, a book, or a movie?

Can you notice some of the interesting changes that come up in these works of art and be more mindful about how interestingly they work together? Take a scene from a movie or literature and notice how the characters shift in thought and feeling, or listen to how the harmonies shift in a piece of music.

Use your artistic watching or listening to refill the creativity well. Now you can begin to notice the connection between your personal and artistic creativity.

Therapeutic Improvisation

IS THIS THING ON?
FINDING YOUR VOICE

My creed for art in general is that it should enrich the soul; it should teach spirituality by showing a person a portion of himself that he would not discover otherwise . . . a part of yourself you never knew existed.

—Jazz pianist Bill Evans

Becoming an Artist

Surrounded by a sea of attendees at *Psychotherapy Networker*'s annual conference, I waited to ask my hero the question that had been burning inside.

One man, with an uncanny resemblance to Sigmund Freud, entranced us yet again with a story of the work we'd all been celebrating and emulating in our own offices for so many years. Our master clinician and storyteller, group therapy guru, and, most importantly, the single most generous and open discloser of his clinical process, Irvin Yalom was reflecting on his lifetime contributions.

It was now our turn to ask him questions.

"Dr. Yalom, you've shown us how to embrace the process and, as poet Rilke advised, to 'be patient toward all that is

1

unsolved in your heart and try to love the questions themselves'"
(Rilke, 1992).

Was I even talking into the microphone? The notes on my
phone bounced out of focus, but I pressed on.

"Like jazz musicians, you've reminded us to enjoy the dissonances and savor the surprises we find within them. Can you
talk about that, the role and importance of being an artist in
our field?"

I was grateful when he acknowledged that yes, he had
thought of calling his book *Letters to a Young Therapist* after
Rilke's famous missives (Rilke, 1992).

"Even though I idolized so many, no, no, I never thought
of myself as an artist. Even though I had wanted to be one, it
wasn't me!"

It was like I had framed the wrong man.

With him ready to quickly move on, I was stunned, stung,
crestfallen. If Yalom couldn't recognize being an artist, how
could any of us?

Luckily for me—and us!—Susan Johnson, the puckish
British couples therapist and our evening's interviewer, held him
up a minute to take stock of his knee-jerk demurral.

Wasn't his work—its graceful storytelling and open embrace
of the therapeutic process—a testament to the power of our art
to heal and enlarge? Was this any less artistic than the poet,
musician, or actor's craft?

Yalom's initial objection ripened into delight on stage, and
after the conference, in a private email, he thanked me, stating
simply, "I'll remember your comment for a very, very long time."

That's what this book is about: the artistry of our work and
how we develop a therapeutic voice to help us get there. This is
vital not only for ourselves and our supervisees but even more
so for our clients, who cultivate their own voice in the interplay
with ours. Happily, there is ample scientific and empirical sup-

port for this artistic venture, and we'll use it to contextualize and illuminate our journey along the way. Although there's a wealth of training for beginning therapists and supervisors, as a profession we neglect and minimize the artistic development—the emerging voice—of the therapist (Cozolino, 2004; Rock, 1997). This chapter defines what a therapeutic voice is, provides an overview of its component parts, and showcases the many practical benefits it has for accelerating treatment progress and building a developing voice for clients on the one hand, and expanding clinician expertise, creativity, and identity development on the other.

Finding Our Voice

All artists—whether writers, musicians, or actors—must develop a voice, that hard-to-define yet distinctive style which runs like an invisible thread through their work, opening up a space of creative possibility between their art and their audience. As a supervisor of early-career clinicians, I view this as essential, playfully likening it to the process of a music teacher fostering the talents of their young protégés.

Just as successful recording artists—seen for instance on the television show *The Voice*—compassionately and thoughtfully mold, mentor, and inspire young talent, so too must we as supervisors help our beginning clinicians. Each has their own music and style they come in playing, and supervisors help them draw out their raw talent, experiment with new genres, and ultimately learn about how to make music that is, as Duke Ellington (Hasse, 1995) said, "beyond category." This is therapy that transcends theoretical orientations, becoming a unique blend of the clinician's theoretical and empirical knowledge, personality, and emerging therapeutic repertoire.

There is a yin and yang here that, when in proper balance and harmony, lead to a fully developed artistic voice. This voice not only serves the therapist, but promotes the opening and expansion of the patient's own voice, becoming the driving force of creative therapeutic work (Lewin, 1997). This also forms the basis for a lifetime of creating art. Yes, all of us therapists—veterans too!—do this daily, in the poetic and musical lines we shape in what others easily pass over as ordinary prose. Freud had it right from the beginning: "When we can share—that is poetry in the prose of life."

Wouldn't it be inspiring if all of us—beginning and veteran clinicians alike, supervisors and supervisees—could embrace the artistry of our everyday work? Wouldn't it be illuminating if we had a working model of how to cultivate and deepen this?

Building a Voice

The model that I've arrived at is both simple yet expansive. A therapeutic voice is the combination and interplay of therapeutic presence and therapeutic authority, the complementary and seemingly contradictory elements that, like yin and yang, enable us to create a three-dimensional picture of our patients and ourselves. Think of it like the way our two eyes, each with their independent perspectives, magically create depth perception.

An ambitious supervisee recently confessed to me, "I have to anticipate everything before our session, and know exactly where I am taking my clients. I feel like a white-water rafting guide who's one turn away from taking the whole crew down with me!"

This supervisee, like so many others, is proficient at being directive, setting goals, and moving quickly toward intervention. Unfortunately, they don't offer enough room for the patient to openly explore and steep in their feelings or draw on the relational process to entertain new possibilities, which is why they so often feel up a creek without a paddle.

Therapeutic Presence

What they need more of is the yin of therapeutic voice—therapeutic presence—the capacity to be receptive, mindfully attentive, emotionally available, nonjudgmental, and resonant with the client's unfolding experience (Geller & Greenberg, 2012). Freud (Freud & Gay, 1995) originated this concept in his earliest recommendation for practicing therapists in 1912, underscoring the vital importance of "evenly hovering attention." Like a koan, the therapist should "simply listen and not bother about whether he is keeping anything in mind" (Freud & Gay, 1995).

Considered the foundation for tuning in to the patient's unconscious, it provided a potent tool for opening up one's mind and heart to new possibilities for understanding and engaging the patient's psyche. Similar to the Zen Buddhist notion of beginner's mind or mindfulness itself (Rubin, 2011; Siegel, 2010), therapeutic presence comes from the framework of "not knowing" in the service of creativity. To paraphrase the Nobel Prize–winning poet Wislawa Szymborska, the point—like the poet's main task—is to say "I don't know" and keep on going (Szymborska et al., 2000). It's to wonder aloud.

Therapeutically present therapists are understanding, openminded, and comfortable with a range of different feelings and perspectives. These therapists have internalized Robert Frost's prescient quip, "No tears in the writer, no tears in the reader. No surprise for the writer, no surprise for the reader" (Frost, 1939; in Barry, 1972). Patients feel a sense of safety, trust, and warmth in their company. The space seems to open up with them. This

disarming quality makes it easy for patients to explore new sub-
plots and turns in their stories. They find themselves surprised at
how much they are saying and learning in just the telling itself.
Therapists who practice this kind of presence don't have
to know immediately and aren't bothered by the ambiguity or
complexity of what they are hearing; they dwell in possibility, as
Emily Dickinson noted in the introduction. They allow patients
to be in the driver's seat so that the patient can show the therapist the territory first, and in so doing, instruct the therapist
how to best be of service. This openness allows all patients to
take more risks in therapy, to deepen the exploration of their
thoughts and feelings, and to truly enjoy the deeper waters of
the psyche, even providing modeling for them to be more open
to the various and contradictory sides of themselves. In short,
to paraphrase Walt Whitman, they are reminded that "We are
large. We contain multitudes."

Owning a Voice

Plopping down in my office chair, and letting out a formidable
sigh, another supervisee recently lamented, "Sometimes I feel
like I'm taking it all in but then can't get a word in edgewise,
and I'm not even sure if what I'm thinking even makes sense.
Am I really helping them at all, or are my own mixed-up feelings
just getting in the way of making any headway?"

I know many fantastic supervisees who excel at being
empathic, reflective, and thoughtful with their patients, but
lack the confidence to make discriminating interpretations and
interventions that take into account their valuable instincts and
intuition regarding new creative possibilities. These supervisees,
understandably, worry that if they use too much of their authority, they will overwhelm or possibly hurt their clients.

Therapeutic Authority

They need more of the yang of therapeutic voice—therapeutic authority—which I define as the command of theory and technique and a discriminating awareness of how to put these into practice. It is the confidence to properly select, apply, time, and adjust one's interventions in a multicultural and relationally sensitive manner (by relying on the yin of therapeutic presence, of course). Moreover, it is the capacity to determine, strategy-wise, which is the right intervention for the right moment: an empathic statement, an incisive question, a cognitive reframe, a deepening articulation of affect, a behavioral rehearsal, or a more nuanced framing of the narrative of self, other, or world.

The therapist with therapeutic authority is happy to show patients how to blaze a new trail, and to empower them to sort through the various aspects of their experience to find bigger patterns and new possibilities. Like an artist mentoring a new student, they can see the bigger and smaller picture and can help with the difficult passages entailed in putting new skills and pieces together.

Most importantly, the therapist with a balanced dose of therapeutic authority knows how to do this with appropriate timing, tact, and empathy. They are not going to break patients down like a drill sergeant, but instead are going to be thoughtfully discriminating and penetrate deeper into problems and their implied solutions.

Supervisory Support

It is vital for supervisors to support beginning clinicians in their developing clinical intuition and instincts, the confident application of their theoretical and empirical knowledge, and a sense for having the authority to make therapeutic moves. Just as a singer needs to take risks with trying out new ways to expand their interpretation of a song, so too does the beginning clinician, and as supervisors, we are right behind them to encourage it.

Supervisors also need to model both how to be comfortable with and how to chase the kind of not-knowing that makes creative therapeutic work possible. Like Yoda to Luke Skywalker, we help them learn how to use the Force, showing them that it is only paradoxically by surrendering and letting go that we truly open up the space for something new to emerge.

Just as our young poet needed Rilke (Corbett, 2016) to learn how to become an artist (and Rilke in turn was mentored by the great sculptor Auguste Rodin), so too do our beginning clinicians need us to illustrate how they can be balanced and integrated in their own unique therapeutic voice by uniting these two crucial faculties. And it turns out that all of us, no matter what level we are at, need to remember that we are always cultivating and expressing this artistry (Lewin, 1997).

Empirically Supported Artistry

Art never needs more than its own justification, but as a scientist practitioner, you might need to be reminded of the scientific support for viewing therapy as an artistic enterprise. Look no further than neuroscientist Antonio Damasio's (2019) book *The Strange Order of Things*, which eloquently showcases the way in which our right-brained artistic feeling comes first, inspiring and motivating our greatest cultural innovations and products, and when joined together with the logic and language of our left brains becomes something truly extraordinary. Daniel Pink (2006) in *A Whole New Mind* illustrates the 21st century's cultural sea change from a left-brain-leaning computer age to a right-brain-leaning conceptual age that integrates right and left to make the best of both worlds.

In his magnum opus, *The Master and His Emissary*, psychiatrist Iain McGilchrist (2009) demonstrates that each hemisphere has its own worldview, reality, and personality, providing a whole different how and why of experiencing and functioning, and that, surprisingly, the right hemisphere does much more work than we give it credit for. More astoundingly, he argues that each hemisphere engages in both cooperative creativity and regular power struggles, each providing the necessary dissonance and consonance that constitute the unique music of the psyche. On the collective level, he argues that this antagonistic complementarity of attending to the world "in two ways at once" has both shaped and been reflected in the philosophy, literature, art, and science of the last two millennia of Western cultural development. But without missing a beat, he demonstrates how this seeming problem leads to an astounding consilience both in our culture and in ourselves. We'll pick up on this theme at the individual level, noting the regular ways in which this right-brain, left-brain battle plays out in our work and the manifold opportunities it simultaneously provides.

In my model, therapeutic presence is the right-brain-dominant aspect of our therapeutic artistry, and therapeutic authority is the left-brain copilot. Therapeutic presence is at once dreamlike and free associative, holistic and big picture, image and metaphor centered, and largely implicit and nonverbal. It undergirds the profound empathic connection between us and our patients, especially to those sides of our clients that have experienced trauma and yet still long for—even in secret—a more redemptive narrative.

Therapeutic authority flows from the language and logic-based sides of our brain with its highly developed executive functioning. More largely conscious and deliberate, this side enables us to zero in and edit the many clinical possibilities before us so that we can work with true specificity and discernment, tailoring our treatment for the unique person sitting across from us, and getting to the heart of the matter. The poem "The Guitarist Tunes Up" by Frances Cornford (1965) sums up this lovely process best. In it, a musician leans into their instrument and courts it with chivalrous delicacy, not commanding or dominating it, but with great sensitivity and respect, preparing to be curious for what music will come from their mutual collaboration. For a visual of this interplay, we can look to none other than that famous Renaissance man—da Vinci and his iconic drawing of his Vitruvian Man. It is only by integrating the square of our logic with the circle of our feelings that we become something truly divine—artists in our own right.

Mindful Creativity

Harvard psychologist Ellen Langer (2005) defines mindful creativity as the process of drawing novel distinctions, what organizational psychologist Adam Grant (2016) playfully terms "vuja de." As we notice new things, she notes, we become aware of how things change depending on the context and perspective from which they are viewed.

In order to be mindfully creative, we need to let go of our fixed mindsets and notice that the stasis of what we are viewing is ironically the stasis of our mindset alone. But the payoff to our lives and work is high: "When we live our lives mindlessly, we don't see, hear, taste, or experience much of what might turn lives verging on boredom into lives that are rich and exciting."

Langer's (1997) empirical research has shown the many tangible rewards of mindful creativity in a variety of domains, from the world of education to public health and beyond. In one study (Langer, 1997), she and her colleagues taught people undergoing major surgery to look at other angles of their hospital experience, to notice some hidden advantages such as having more time to be in touch with family, reexamine their life goals, or even their forced weight loss. Patients in this mindful group showed lower stress levels, took fewer pain medications, and left the hospital sooner than those in the nonmindful condition.

Langer (1997) champions a counterintuitive approach to mastering a craft. Instead of viewing diversions or digressions as mere distractions, she notes their potential as "being otherwise attracted" and often as harbingers of creative innovation. In lieu of the overly regimented and dogmatic "practice makes perfect" mentality, she shows that consciously varying one's practice makes for a much more productive, meaningful, and enjoyable road toward proficiency in one's chosen field. Langer is showing us that the therapeutic voice we are seeking is the product of an open receptivity and willingness to vary on the one hand, and the capacity to notice and draw novel distinctions on the other.

Mindful Creativity in Action

Joy Mangano, as played by Jennifer Lawrence in the 2015 film *Joy*, is an unconscious collector of broken things (Russel et al., 2015). In an early scene, her self-absorbed father Rudy, played by Robert De Niro, is returned home to her like a dog.

"I don't want him anymore. He's damaged. He's been living in my house for 2 years," the neighbor confesses.

Joy doesn't know where to put him. Her singer-wannabee ex-husband is staying in her basement, and just as Rudy makes his way to locate a potential room of his own, he encounters his ex-wife. A soap opera–obsessed, *Glass Menagerie* figurine, she passive-aggressively lashes into him, questioning why his new girlfriend and her Metropolitan Museum tastes are better than hers.

"Museums are for dust and death," she taunts as she moves like lightning to dub him Captain Jack. Rudy unknowingly takes the bait and is slugged with her self-satisfied grin as she tells him it is short for Captain Jackass.

Finally rattled, Rudy now goes for her jugular and says it's like being in a crazy house talking with her. He compares her to a gas leak: "We don't smell you and see you, but you are killing us all!" Not long after, a glass vase is thrown and Joy, as usual, is the one to clean up the mess.

In another similar scene after celebrating the launch of a boat, Joy is left to mop up the shards of a champagne bottle and bloodies her hands. It is at that moment of mindful creativity when the vision of the self-wringing mop arrives, when Joy is at once liberated from her mindless role of victim into a self-styled Daedalus inventor.

Everything is the same. Joy again is in the role of dealing with the mess, brokenness, and damage found in the wake of her family's dysfunction, but, in a moment of mindful creativity, she envisions a new angle. This is her ticket out. She can now reclaim the Joy that is hers.

Learning and Teaching From Art

If we are to find and develop a therapeutic voice, we must first look at how therapy itself connects to the arts and how, as supervisors and supervisees, we can attend to these important dimensions. We'll look specifically to poetry and music as starting points.

POETRY LESSONS

A sonnet is a type of poem that compresses a question or problem, its exploration, and a final statement of some revelation or new understanding into 14 lines. In Shakespeare's (2002) famous sonnet "Shall I compare thee to a summer's day?" the speaker wrestles back and forth with how his love is and is not like summer. Initially, it seems very fitting to compare her to the beauty and splendor of the season, but upon further inspection, new ideas emerge. Among other things, she is much more constant, evenly tempered, reliable, and more lovely than the summer months.

Much like Shakespeare's speaker, we wrestle with our initial diagnostic impressions of our patients: Shall I compare thee to a borderline personality, a depressive, or an adjustment disorder? It is not immediately clear, and so much of our first sessions entail testing out various hypotheses to determine who the patient is and is not.

As Shakespeare's poem continues, surprises and new discoveries emerge, and toward the final turn of the poem, the poet concludes that his love will be eternal as a result of the poetic act itself: "So long as men can breathe or eyes can see / so long lives this, and this gives life to thee" (Shakespeare, 2002, p. 417). This is the ultimate aim of a transformative therapeutic process. Much like a sonnet, by the end of the therapeutic experience, a patient will be able to make a few turns and come to a way of internalizing the therapeutic process so that it too will become eternal.

MUSIC LESSONS

Beethoven's 1808 Fifth Symphony provides an immediately recognizable compressed musical idea. In only four notes, a focal theme is established that is explored, varied, and reharmonized in much the same way that occurs in therapy. The capacity of the therapist to articulate that melody—the dominant trend or relational pattern that pulls the various strands of a patient's story together—goes very far in clarifying what has been troubling patients at the same time that it points in the direction of how they can move forward. Much of the time, patients are playing the notes of their issues but are not aware of the melody and cannot synthesize it into a focal theme. They bring us their own invisible scores, hoping that we will give them feedback to be able to recognize their own music.

About seven and a half minutes into the third movement of Rachmaninoff's 1908 Symphony in E minor, we hear the main theme played by the French horn, in the manner that a patient initially expresses when it is recognized by the counselor: "You hear me! This is the song I didn't know I was singing." Shortly after, the theme gets played by the violin with a melancholy poignancy: "I have been waiting a long time suffering with this alone." This is the sense of sadness and mourning that the patient feels for having had to sequester this aspect of self in the service of protection and adaptation.

As the theme gets worked upon and elaborated, new instruments, such as the oboe and flute, come in to take on the line, with hope gathering. Calmer and with greater poise, a certain pride and expressiveness opens up now that this very significant idea can be incorporated into the larger musical narrative of the patient's story.

Let's see how this artistry translates to a representative case and get a preview of putting all of the pieces together. Throughout the rest of the book, we'll zoom in on each facet of this therapeutic voice to help you or your supervisee integrate this more personally.

A Case of You

I've named this "A Case of You" as a nod to Joni Mitchell's heartbreakingly beautiful song because this patient seemed at first blush like she was too much to handle. Pretty quickly in our first session, I realized that, as for so many of our cases, I really liked and admired her for her pluckiness and fire. And even more importantly, it surprised me that I could hold on and remain standing as I imbibed her powerful mix of spirits. A first-year student came to her intake appointment complaining that her friends did not understand her, that she couldn't fathom why they were so turned off by the razor blade that she kept on her desk as a reminder that she could cut herself, and that she had been told to come to counseling many times but it had never been helpful in the past. She asked, why should she bother now?

Prior counselors had told her that she needed a higher level of care than they could provide, and those appointments left the student feeling misunderstood and blamed for troubles she too could not fathom. She also felt a sense of hopelessness at not being able to make true contact, just as she had not with family and friends.

Aiming right for the jugular, she also scoffed at me: "Counselors are incompetent and don't really understand me. You probably won't either!"

In addition to feeling interpersonally rejected on a number of fronts, as a first-generation college student, she experienced the pressure of well-meaning parents who hoped to see the family's metaphorical stock rise with her success. At the same time, her family expected her to be at the ready when they called her to take care of her younger siblings. She was a painter who loved the darkest colors of her palette, with her works centering on Hopperesque misfits wandering in the night.

Initially, her cutting was a regular strategy to express and modulate her emotions, combined with a preoccupation with death, and the ways in which friends and other therapists had been repelled by her behavior made me wonder whether this student had borderline personality disorder. As in Shakespeare's poem, though, I was not sure whether this comparison truly fit.

Here we see the internal wrestling of therapeutic authority and presence. Our first attempt at wielding therapeutic authority can let us all too quickly categorize or even pathologize what we are seeing before we get the full story. The left brain often likes to get in the action first and demonstrate its superior language and logic. At the same time, this discriminating faculty provides crucial information that we really need to follow. Like a samurai warrior, psychologically speaking, we need to forge the sword of our left-brain therapeutic authority and learn how to use it appropriately. Toggling back and forth between this function and therapeutic presence—the open and receptive right-brained Buddha nature—allows us both to see the big picture clearly and to focus keenly on the supporting details we need to assess and intervene incisively.

As I got to know more about the patient's relational backdrop and leaned into my therapeutic presence, things looked a bit different. I learned about her parents' difficulty tolerating fear, anger, and sadness and their own struggles with managing chronically high levels of stress. I also learned about the many times and ways her family was unable to acknowledge or stay with her emotional experience.

Just as the subject of the Shakespearean poem was no longer so much like the summer, it seemed more and more that she was no longer like a patient with a borderline organization and instead more like one with a neurotic organization or a possible adjustment disorder. She appeared to be in a conflict that could not be acknowledged squarely as she was in the midst of an important developmental transition, both issues coloring each other and placing her in an ever-tightening Gordian knot.

As I trusted my therapeutic authority, a focal theme emerged. When this patient expressed negative emotions, people could not tolerate them and emotionally and physically abandoned her. This pattern was consistent with her emerging friendships—others were not interested in hanging out with her despite her charm and intelligence—and also extended to her early family experience, in which her parents subjected her to the silent treatment for days whenever her emotions ran too hot. Taken together, the patient internalized a message that her emotions were problematic and disruptive and that they must be put aside and suppressed. In other words, they became "not-me" and funneled into the dissociative symptom of cutting.

Until I was able to hone in on a focal theme, I, like the therapists before me, was part of the problem, imagining in my countertransference that it was the patient who had the major issue. Internally, I underestimated how much my feelings were part of an enactment, containing only a small piece of the story. Initially, I was bracing myself for difficult work, assuming that the student had a great deal of pathology and would make little movement. In a way, I was reenacting the dynamic of the student's relational backdrop, finding her issues disruptive to my sense of authority, just as they did for her parents and prior therapists—"It's not me, it's her." As I maintained a therapeutically present stance, this crucial dynamic was able to be observed and incorporated into a new understanding and relationship with the client.

Therapeutic authority led me to a focal theme that helped me see that it was totally understandable for her to shy away from sharing her intense feelings and needing to hide and express it in her not-so-secret ritual of cutting. She was protecting both myself and herself from not-me and also letting the world know, with what seemed to be twisted pride, that cutting was her right and a very valuable part of her emotional life. Looking back on that detail now, it was very prescient in the way it encapsulated her attempt to express and independently resolve her bind.

Tracking the Changes

Guided by a mindful application of therapeutic presence, and a discriminating use of therapeutic authority, the first-year student went through the kind of musical sequence referenced above. Initially, having a therapist who was able to respect and receive the fullness of her experience without mistreating or abandoning her by becoming critical or explosive or falling apart was a tremendous step toward a new relational experience. The recognition that her focal theme was understandable and heard enabled her to begin to speak of it without the kind of shame and dissociation that often accompanies a not-me experience. It also enabled her to begin to trust and hope again.

She became inwardly and outwardly relaxed so that she could begin to examine the many facets of her current and past experience and thus begin the riffing that is essential to the jazz improvisation that is therapy. In short, she began to find and develop her own voice as a patient.

The patient was able to view her behaviors as more comprehensible and expressive of the hidden conflicts she had been harboring and that had been left unformulated and disconnected (Stern, 2009). This expanding sense of self-compassion became an important antidote to her cutting behavior and provided an alternative avenue for exploring and containing her emotional experience. Interpersonally, she became less defensive and fearful of others abandoning her, having had a transformative set of experiences in which she felt the consistent presence of a reliable other. She began to show her pain not only in her words but in the artwork she did as a painter.

The Turn of the Poem

When a poetic turn or musical theme has been established, shifts can immediately be seen in the patient and felt in the relationship. These can occur simply in the change of posture (often, a straightening of the back and sitting up in one's chair), a richer tone of voice, a feeling of newfound connection and space in the therapeutic relationship, or in the spontaneity and flow of narrative or images that emerge in the therapeutic interplay. For clinicians, who are more accustomed to tracking numerical data, a good barometer for these changes can be found in Counseling Center Assessment of Psychological Symptoms (CCAPS-34) data (Martin et al., 2012).

As can be seen in Table 1.1, the patient's scores began to show changes from the very second session. In the first session, trust was developed as the student began to see me as a figure who could understand and appreciate the depth of her pain and recognize the myriad ways in which she had been misjudged and pigeonholed by her family, friends, and, most notably, other therapists. We also developed a focal theme centering on the ways in which this rejection had led her to suppress and negate her very important and precious feelings. Taken together, I believe that these turns led to decreased scores in hostility and distress, each indicative of the fact that she was feeling more trusting, less defensive, and relieved at being able to begin to experience her emotions more directly.

These scores continued to remain significantly lower than baseline for the next few sessions, whereupon we worked on developing ways of shifting these patterns in her relationships with friends and family. At around session five, the student's depression scores started to decrease as she began to feel greater self-efficacy and agency in being able to effect change in her life inside and outside of the therapy space.

TABLE 1.1 Counseling Center Assessment of Psychological Symptoms (CCAPS-34) Data for Sample Student.

SUBSCALE	SESSION 1 BASELINE	SESSION 2	SESSION 3	SESSION 4
Depression	99	94	94	91
Generalized anxiety	95	90	90	90
Social anxiety	95	85	89	85
Academic distress	83	43↓[1]	57	49
Eating concerns	39	57	57	57
Hostility	94	51↓[1]	58↓[1]	64↓[1]
Alcohol use	46	56	56	76
Distress index	99	83↓[1]	87↓[1]	86↓[1]
SI/HI	4/0	3/0	3/0	3/0

NOTE. Arrows indicate a statistically significant change in score. The number following indicates the standard deviation of change. SI/HI = suicidal/homicidal ideation.

SOURCE: From Michael D. Alcée & Tara A. Sager (2017). How to Fall in Love With Time-Limited Therapy: Lessons From Poetry and Music, Journal of College Student Psychotherapy. Reprinted by permission of the publisher (Taylor & Francis Ltd, http://www.tandfonline.com).

Simultaneously, her levels of anxiety followed suit as they made a statistically significant drop from baseline in our final session of the semester.

These data concretize the notion of making a more poetic and musical line in our therapeutic work with patients and highlight the importance of drawing on artistic metaphors to inform

SESSION 5	SESSION 6	SESSION 7	SESSION 8	SESSION 9	SESSION 10
85↓[1]	85↓[1]	85↓[1]	85↓[1]	89↓[1]	73↓[1]
90	83	83	83	83	71↓[1]
85	85	85	80	85	80
70	57	57	63	70	57
65	65	65	65	65	65
58↓[1]	64↓[1]	58↓[1]	64↓[1]	74↓[1]	69↓[1]
76	76	76	76	76	76
86↓[1]	80↓[1]	80↓[1]	82↓[1]	86↓[1]	71↓[1]
2/0	2/1	2/0	2/0	2/0	2/0

SOURCE: Michael D. Alcée & Tara A. Sager (2017). How to Fall in Love With Time-Limited Therapy: Lessons From Poetry and Music, Journal of College Student Psychotherapy. Reprinted by permission of the publisher (Taylor & Francis Ltd, http://www.tandfonline.com).

treatment and expand both the therapist's and patient's voices in that process.

A New Slant on Working Dynamically

We are very accustomed as clinicians to thinking vertically, troubling ourselves over quick diagnoses and assessments, especially given the limited time we often have. At some points, this may take away from focusing horizontally on the musical line and the movement of the intervention. In music, in order to play or sing a melody successfully, one needs to be as attentive to the horizontal motion of the notes carrying a melodic line forward as to the vertical axis of hitting the note itself.

In clinical practice, one can analogize the horizontal forward motion to the momentum of an intervention, the movement toward a new relational experience. The vertical playing of the note is the clinical equivalent of making sure you are understanding the patient's experience correctly and getting a proper diagnostic read. The horizontal motion is informed by therapeutic presence just as, conversely, the vertical movement is guided by therapeutic authority. Both are essential, and they need to be worked in concert in order to turn notes into music.

This musical way of approaching relational work helps us to be more efficient, fluid, and creative, focusing simultaneously on how to skillfully assess and intervene in our fast-paced culture. Moreover, it enables us to carry the themes of the patient's past into new orchestrations and harmonizations in the present, providing a model for continued transformative possibilities in the future. Through this process, patients internalize working creatively with their own themes and then take us into new melodic and harmonic territory, stimulating further treatment progress and development. Taken together, this fosters a positive feedback loop in the creative matrix between patient and therapist, and from this synergy, transformative changes quickly follow.

This is precisely what a well-tuned therapeutic voice does for us, and that's what we'll build in the rest of the pages that follow.

Why Artistry Is Needed Now
in the 21st Century

In his prescient book *A Whole New Mind: Why Right-Brainers Will Rule the Future*, Daniel Pink (2006) illustrates that economically and culturally, we have moved from an information age to a conceptual age, one that marries meaning and aesthetics to technical expertise and innovation. But even more powerfully, he lays out a call to arms to those who seek to be successful and fulfilled in the 21st century, saying, "The wealth of nations and the well-being of individuals now depend on having *artists in the room*. In a world enriched by abundance but disrupted by automation and outsourcing of white-collar work, everyone, regardless of profession, must cultivate an *artistic sensibility*" (emphasis added).

Organizational psychologist Adam Grant (2016) echoes the value of incorporating creativity and artistry into our professional lives, focusing on the importance of moving beyond the default mode and embracing vuja de, the capacity to be curious about why the default exists in the first place and how we can envision new possibilities in old problems. He illustrates the tangible outcomes of this with a study by economist Michael Housman, who found that just the choice of internet browser predicted workers who were more committed and better performing. Moreover, he shows how startups like Warby Parker became the "Netflix of eyeglasses" by artistically reimagining a way of finding new solutions but, more importantly, of asking really good questions.

The artistic sensibility that asks and embraces these questions is at the heart of this book's purpose, providing the compass by which to find that therapeutic voice which is uniquely yours. Now, let's discover it together again.

EXERCISE 1: Therapeutic Presence or Therapeutic Authority: Which Is My Dominant Side? (True or False)

1. —— I enjoy allowing the process to unfold and being surprised by what there is to explore together.

2. —— I like to have techniques at the ready to help my clients find relief and develop long-term strategies for wellness.

3. —— I like letting feelings steep for a bit so I get a better sense of what is happening inside my client's emotional world.

4. —— I enjoy honing in on a central theme or interpretation to help a client clarify the seeming chaos of their experience.

5. —— I like being in the role of the expert like an omniscient narrator seeing more than the client themselves.

6. —— I find it stimulating and energizing to be temporarily lost and not fully knowing yet what is happening in the room when I'm working with a client.

7. —— I like working with clients who have clear diagnoses that are readily amenable to treatment interventions.

8. —— I enjoy working with clients who are more challenging, complex, and don't fit in any particular box.

9. —— I feel very confident sharing my own clinical intuition or even using my self-disclosure in the service of helping my clients.

10. —— I often feel and think a lot of things about my clients, but I don't feel comfortable intruding on their process.

ASSESSING YOURSELF

If you marked questions 1, 3, 6, 8, or 10 as true, then you show stronger signs of therapeutic presence as your more dominant side. It is especially likely if you endorsed three or more of these questions as true and if you answered "false" to questions 2, 4, 5, 7, or 9.

Kelly endorsed questions 1, 3, and 10 as true and 2, 4, 5, and 9 as false. She has a more natural preference for her right-brain-driven therapeutic presence, feeling much more at home in observing and facilitating her client's process, so much so that she worries about intruding on it too much. She feels less naturally comfortable with owning her authority and expertise and doesn't yet feel as empowered to express more fully her very clear therapeutic gifts. She will as she uses Chapter 5 to learn how to take on her therapeutic authority.

If you marked questions 2, 4, 5, 7, or 9 as true, then you show stronger signs of therapeutic authority as your more dominant side. It is especially likely if you endorsed three or more of these questions and you answered false to questions 1, 3, 6, 8, or 10.

Alexander endorsed 2, 4, 5, and 7 as true and 1, 3, 6, and 10 as false. He instinctively feels much more comfortable with mobilizing his left-brain-driven therapeutic authority, enjoying the structured, goal-oriented, and highly active and explicit ways he can help his clients grow and improve. He feels less confident and secure in his capacity to allow the process to unfold, to steep more deeply in affect, and trust himself when he feels like he doesn't know where he is taking his clients or how to best implement prepared rather than improvisational interventions. He will be greatly helped by Chapter 4.

If you are evenly developed in your therapeutic presence and authority, you are more likely to have endorsed a relatively equal number of questions from both sides. For example, if you endorsed every question as true except number 10, you are very likely to have a highly integrated and evenly balanced therapeutic voice.

Caroline endorsed 1, 2, 3, 4, 7, 8, and 9 as true and 5, 6, and 10 as false. She feels equally comfortable facilitating and following her client's and her own process, panning out or zooming in with discriminating interventions and techniques, sharing her self-disclosure in the service of client growth, and working with both clear and complex cases. With experience under her belt, she confided in me that she started out as a therapist with more dominant therapeutic presence—as illustrated by her longtime interest in meditation practice—and found ways of integrating that with her own therapeutic authority using techniques and interventions that deepened the process and facilitated better outcomes for her clients.

Don't worry if you lean one way or the other at first. It is typical to have a dominant side, much as a musician is dominant in either technique or expressivity at first, or like a pianist who has either their right or left hand as their stronger player. It is the goal to capitalize on the strengths of your dominant side and to lean into developing your less dominant side so you are on the road to fashioning a distinctive voice that is flexible, confident, and effective. We'll have more case examples and strategies for strengthening your therapeutic presence and authority in the chapters to come.

EXERCISE 2: Why Do I Lean Toward Therapeutic Presence or Authority?

There are many reasons that therapists lean toward one side or the other of their therapeutic voice.

1. WHAT'S YOUR NATURE?

Sometimes, it's a nature thing, a matter of temperament or personality, with some being more geared toward the introverted, introspective, and feeling side of therapeutic presence or others toward the more extroverted, action-oriented, thinking side of therapeutic authority.

Many therapists are empaths or highly sensitive persons (HSPs), which may lean them more naturally toward therapeutic presence, monitoring, containing, and regulating the environment for their clients in the ways they are accustomed to do for themselves and others by default (Aron, 1996). For these therapists, it takes more practice to guide that empathy and sensitivity toward the self. We all know that many therapists talk about self-care as an afterthought in much of their speaking and writing, and even as a field we are often guilty of forgetting ourselves too easily. In addition, it may take more deliberate practice (Levenson, 2021; Rousmaniere, 2016) and coaching to remember that taking on their therapeutic authority can be very helpful not just for their clients, but also for their fuller agency, self-efficacy, and enjoyment as therapists.

There are also many therapists who gravitate to and love the field because of the perpetual quest to figure out what makes us tick, to understand, analyze, and work out the mechanisms that help clients get back to optimal functioning. They are very inclined to the scientific enterprise that undergirds therapeutic authority, the deliberate and discriminating implementation of proven strategies for greater emotional well-being and integration. They may feel more confident and secure in this arena while feeling somewhat suspect and uncomfortable about trusting the more right-brained experiential side of therapeutic presence. Again, deliberate practice (Levenson, 2021; Rousmaniere, 2016) and encouragement in trusting and strengthening their therapeutic presence will help them to see how much it can add and complement their therapeutic authority.

2. WHAT'S YOUR NURTURE?

Sometimes, it is a nurture thing, where our preferred style is an identification or counteridentification with important figures in our family of origin or in our culture, and a desire to either honor a legacy or not repeat a problematic or dysfunctional one.

If, for example, you grew up with an overbearing, micromanaging, or critical mother or father and absolutely hated it, you might want to be as receptive as Carl Rogers learned to be from growing up in a fairly repressive household where he wasn't allowed to chew gum or dance.

If you grew up in a far too permissive house without enough stabilizing rules or a sense of true guidance, you may have developed the counteridentification of being a steadying captain, intent on making sure others are safe and secure and not just fending for themselves in what feels like a chaotic world.

It could also be a positive identification with a parent, teacher, or hero from a book or movie that inspires your particular leaning. And as we'll see, it's often a hero that attempts to combine both that we truly love. For me, it was Atticus Finch, the hero of Harper Lee's *To Kill a Mockingbird* (Lee, 2006), who embodied how to be compassionately present and receptive and yet also confident and articulate in his authority and what he stood for.

Who are some of the heroes—within the field of therapy or outside of it—you admired and modeled yourself after?

3. WHAT'S YOUR METATHEORETICAL FRAMEWORK?

Sometimes your leaning is connected to a particular theoretical orientation that appeals or has deep resonance for you, whether that be humanistic, cognitive-behavioral, dialectical-behavioral, dynamic, gestalt, existential, acceptance and commitment, or any number of theories brought together in their own distinctive combination. This metatheoretical framework expresses, contains, and guides your therapeutic values and is foundational to who you are as a therapist. For example, for those more aligned with humanistic therapy, therapeutic presence will likely be their go-to strength, whereas those with a behavioral stance are more likely to operate from their therapeutic authority first.

1. What are the ways in which your natural leaning fits with your temperament?

   _____

   _____

   _____

2. What are the ways in which your natural leaning flows from your experience? Are there any particular identifications or counteridentifications that inspire that leaning?

   _____

   _____

   _____

3. What are the ways in which your natural leaning expresses or aligns with your metatheoretical orientation?

   _____

   _____

   _____

RIGHTING THE LEFT BRAIN: NEUROSCIENCE MAKES ARTISTS OUT OF US

The left brain has gotten a lot of airtime. Along with the frontal lobe, it's been the main story for human beings, our raison d'être, claim to fame, and go-to default. It makes sense. The left brain and its magnificent logic and language have smooth talked us for years: "Who would you even *be* without me?" Like a jealous lover, the left brain has made that romantic mess of a right brain feel like it would be lost and penniless on its own.

If you haven't already noticed, I'm using the oldest therapist trick in the book: modeling. I'm showing what is important for you to take in and internalize for us to connect and communicate more fully together. In the paragraph above, I've used metaphor, humor, and shameless attempts at communicating directly with your right brain. Why? Because this chapter is going to highlight how effective and transformational these capacities are for us as fully realized and integrated human beings and how central they are to the creative work we do improvising with our patients.

And of course modeling—to quote former President Barack Obama sinking a three-pointer from downtown—that's just what we do! Built into our DNA and mirror neurons, we are meant to connect by feeling and sharing what we have seen and felt around us in our relationships.

As relational therapists, this is even more crucial, as modeling—especially the modeling that takes Texas-sized emotional and intellectual risks—is the muse for so much of our work. We demonstrate the leaps of faith necessary to make new feelings, thoughts, and whole narratives possible.

Like great actors, we embody the fullest scope of the character sitting before us—including their most unsavory, misunderstood, or juvenile features—and express them back in the most poignant, three-dimensional ways so our patients can begin to see and love themselves again. Even better, they naturally become motivated to pay themselves and us back with new creative risks themselves; they invest in their fullest humanity again.

Modeling incorporates mirroring, deeply taking in the range of what we pick up emotionally and cognitively and putting it out there as a new form, a new shared mode of communication. Improvisation often starts with repeating someone else's lick, but then the creativity comes when we vary it just enough to make it interesting for us to play anew together.

The right brain is the neuroscientific base camp from which the fireworks display of our everyday emotions originates—remember all those lightning-fast changes we talked about in the introduction? The right brain is fastest to pick up those changes and signals from others too: it is the central command for our internal Department of Empathy. Exquisitely responsive and discriminating at recognizing faces, feelings, and tone, it is best equipped and positioned to lead us in our aims at therapeutic improvisation.

But let's not swell the right brain's head too much and overcompensate; we are just here to *right* the left brain in order to be artistic, innovative, and effective as therapists. Our task is to integrate and strengthen the connections between the right brain and left brain, understanding how to optimize, honor, and respect their strengths. Along the way, it's crucial to know their limitations and, most interestingly, how we human beings, like the biblical Jacob, are built to fight and wrestle with ourselves all the time in the service of something larger.

Put broadly, our mission is to realign the connection between our right and left brain at the individual and collective level. Because as Antonio Damasio (2019) and many others have pointed out, Descartes both freed and trapped us with his famous formulation "I think, therefore I am." Why? Because contemporary neuroscience is showing us that it is more accurate to say, "I feel a lot and think I know what I don't fully know yet, therefore I am."

It's no wonder why Puck, the mischievous fairy in Shakespeare's *Midsummer Night's Dream* who both watches and manipulates humans to fall foolishly in love with the wrong person, declares, "Lord, what fools these mortals be!" Without a whole-brain understanding of ourselves, we and our patients do all sorts of foolish things. We say we want one thing and do another; we grasp for the wrong people to heal our troubled past or turn those loving people who *can* heal us into those who can't again, and we shame ourselves for not being smarter about how foolish we all are at our very core.

But thank goodness, to echo poet laureate Billy Collins's poem "Nightclub," we are all such beautiful fools. Riffing on the jazz standard "You Are Too Beautiful," (Rodgers and Hart, 1932) Collins circles around the fact that we all feel so foolish to be in love, yet hardly ever say that we are so beautiful and others are fools to be in love with us. Instead, we sit mesmerized, listening to somebody else play our song.

At the climax of Collins's poem, the speaker, a representative of the Everyman, is plucked out of the audience by the saxophone player and granted the opportunity to take matters into his own hands. His bebop solo proclaims what we so often feel but rarely say, all of us, "—so damn foolish, we have become beautiful without even knowing it." In other words, if we take a closer look at how we're built, we too are capable of even greater beauty and possibility than we initially realize.

This is the goal of therapeutic improvisation: to make a more beautiful form out of the seeming mess of confusing thoughts and capricious feelings we all carry, bobble, drop, and catch in this funny process of being fully human.

A Whole-Brain Approach: On Feeling, Mindsight, and Meaning

Neuroscientist Antonio Damasio (2019) agrees that feelings have not gotten their proper due and credit "as motives, monitors, and negotiators of human cultural endeavours." At best, feelings are relegated to best supporting actor in an ensemble cast, and at worst, they are considered irrational frills that get in the way of the serious work of showcasing our superiority as human beings.

But Damasio insists that these feelings jump-started and propelled the cultural innovations in the arts, sciences, and everything else in between that have made us so special in the first place. Even more so, feelings form the origin story of our creative world.

It's true that language, logic, and social savoir faire implement and execute much of this extraordinary work, but feelings motivate it, regulate it, and, best of all, make the creative adjustments necessary to keep things moving. They are the improviser par excellence in all of us, much like the bird of hope that, Emily Dickinson (1976a) notes, persistently sings in all of us.

From bacteria to worker bees and ants on upward to humans, Damasio contends that feeling supplies an intelligence and the motive that moves us.

How We Are Built

So how can we hold on to these slippery feelings and thoughts that course through us? Consummate teachers of neuroscience to professionals and the layperson, Dan Siegel and Tina Payne Bryson make it easy for us to grasp our metaphorical brain in hand with an alliterative pneumonic. The left brain, they tell us, "is *logical, literal* (it likes words), and *linear* (it puts things in a sequence or order). The left brain *loves* that all four of these words begin with the letter L. (It also loves lists)" (Siegel & Bryson, 2012).

The right brain, with a mind of its own, prefers to be holistic, dreamy, intuitive, and emotional. Even though it is largely nonverbal, it likes to get personal and draw from a deep reservoir of autobiographical memories, emotions, and images. It also loves to see and interpret you personally, again taking in those light-speed changes appearing in the microexpressions in your face and in your eyes, the window to your soul. It loves to pick up the nuanced music of your shifting tone—what is called prosody—and to contextualize it with all the feedback you get from your lower brain and even further south in your body, in your heart and gut.

Allan Schore's work makes the most persuasive case that the art of psychotherapy flows straight from the science of interpersonal neurobiology, that the thorniest and most intriguing aspects of our work come from the way we are built and meant to function as part of our dazzling humanity. As therapists and artists, Schore (2019) notes, we are constantly toggling back and forth between these two channels: the implicit, unconscious, nonverbal right brain and the explicit, conscious, verbal left brain. The right brain falls into reverie and paws its way closer to the beating heart of the conversation we're sharing as the left brain attempts to analyze and prepare its response as if it were completing a puzzle; the left brain then consults again with the right before it makes a move.

Schore notes that our key job as therapists is to help our clients recalibrate and reclaim their capacity to self-regulate and improvise more effectively by speaking first from our right brains directly to theirs. This gets underneath left-brain-oriented defenses and inhibitions that can be so antagonistic to new experience, especially for those who have been shaped and conditioned by trauma and necessary dissociation (Herman, 1997; Kalsched, 1996).

This right-brain-led approach opens up a safer potential space that emerges in the relationship itself, mirroring the maternal bond that initially formed the capacity to connect, attach, and improvise in the first place. Known as the American Bowlby, Schore champions the centrality of the relationship as the emotional conductor that oversees our multiplicity—the various sides of self that are constantly changing and looking for safe and creative expression—and provides a reliable internal metronome to keep up with the difficult music we find ourselves so often playing.

The Master and His Emissary

With extraordinary depth and breadth, psychiatrist Iain McGilchrist (2009) counts the ways of the right hemisphere's singular gifts, dubbing it the master—I prefer "the maestro"—who relies on the left hemisphere as its special emissary and diplomat. Not only is the right brain online first in development and more involved than the left brain in growth of the self as a "social empathic being," it also originated earlier phylogenetically in our evolution as a species.

More deeply embedded in and linked to the limbic and autonomic systems, the right brain is faster and more accurate than the left brain at emotional comprehension, specializes in the recognition of faces and places, revels in personal connections with individuals in the real versus the abstracted world, and gleans with stunning accuracy a person's physiognomy, voice, gait, and individuality.

Because the right brain is so embodied, emotional, and enamored of relationships, it is also the source of the literal and figurative music and improvisation so essential for our work as therapists. Even more poignantly, the right brain is much more in tune with sadness compared to anger, and is consequently much better equipped at the working through and healing process necessary for effective therapy.

If that wasn't already enough for our important task as therapists, the right brain is also the master at the kinds of sweeping and specific attention that allows us to deeply explore and open up new possible understandings and emotional experiences, to keep up with those many changes we've been tracking. And even better, the right is impeccable at the quicksilver frame and set shifts that enable us to improvise on new material without losing our place in the music. It relishes the hidden dissonances and discrepancies that it uses to rethink its original conception and keep on improvising anew.

Bromberg (2006) writes about Jean Charcot, the great neurologist, playfully capping off a verbal duel with a young Freud with a fantastic zinger: "Theory is good but it doesn't prevent things from existing." The right brain never loses track of this fact, and is, like a good fiction reader, ever willing to suspend disbelief, to see what things actually are and where they can possibly go. The right brain doesn't reify the impersonal category but instead stays both grounded and hovering in the service of the great human mystery: the dynamic interplay of the changes that make up our perpetual and most personal improvisations.

The right brain also has no preconceptions. It is a master at being a novice, hungrily learning new information, skills, and even verbal material without an egotistical sense of ownership. Constantly aware of and holding on to the whole, the right brain has a magnificent integrative power that is fueled by its constant search for and recognition of patterns. It is always on the scene when there's novelty and new possibility, even in the case of language itself.

You might protest that the right brain is relatively silent and inferior in terms of language production, but keep in mind, it studies and tracks among the most interesting and important features of language itself: tone, meaning, metaphor, and humor. In short, it deals with everything that captures the stunning multiplicity of our selves (Lehrer, 2008), providing the ever-shifting contextual scenery that helps us make sense of the where, what, and why of the human monologues and dialogues on life's metaphorical stage.

Even in its supposed weak suit—the verbal sphere—the right brain has a remarkable capacity to range far and wide in its associations of words, calling forth words from seemingly distant lands and contexts, in order to fully fathom ourselves in relationship. To illustrate their differing modes, McGilchrist (2009) contrasts the way the right and left brain approach and deal with the meaning of the color red. The left sees red primarily in the red traffic light for its abstract impersonal rule and its explicit usefulness, while the right brain sees red in the rose, the possible symbol for some of the greatest and most novel poetic possibilities.

Not sold on the right brain's extraordinariness? Consider this amazing fact: McGilchrist shares that there is a near-universal tendency for babies to be cradled on the left side so that the right brain can do its stunning work of emotionally tuning in, because that way the baby is exposed to the parent's left hemiface, the right-brain-controlled area that has been shown to be the most expressive, nuanced, and improvisatory half of the human face. Even if, as a parent, you are a lefty, this is the side which is favored because nature knows how skilled the right side truly is. Relationally, then, we all start from the right side.

The left brain, in contrast, can be so narrowly, impersonally, and categorically focused that without the right hemisphere it will literally neglect a whole side of vision even if it has the physical capacity to see it. Despite its seeming limits on its own and the ways it has been overvalued in culture since science became dominant, the left brain is our most important and faithful ally. It enables us to control, manipulate, predict, and bring into usable focus our often kaleidoscopic world and uses the special gifts of language and abstraction themselves to make us true agents of our own destiny; without our left hemisphere, we would be awash in experience and adrift in understanding.

McGilchrist is right; the left brain is our true emissary, speaking for us and from us with precision, power, and perspicacity. It has the miraculous capacity "to 'unpack' experience. Without its distance and structure, certainly there could be, for example, no art, only experience" (McGilchrist, 2009, p. 199).

As a simple metaphor to make sense of it, the right brain functions much like the gas pedal on a car. It gives you quick momentum and takes you places far and fast, and yet it would be nothing without the left brain, which functions as the brake. The left brain uses its discriminating reason to slow us down when we're about to crash and even makes sure we are able to take the turns of everyday life. It is inhibitory for a life-saving and enhancing purpose; without it, we wouldn't be able to follow the directions and get to the destinations we say we want to go to.

The left brain has the necessary chops to analyze and "re-present" the world for us in an intelligible and discriminating way—much like our therapeutic authority—and only then does it pass our perception on to the right brain once again so that the world can live again and be harmonized and unified through the miraculous power of our creative imagination (Kalsched, 2013).

McGilchrist analogizes us to musicians who must break down the components of the musical score in our practice in order to reunite them again in performance. It is no wonder then why we need to be such good improvisers! This is how we operate in therapy as in life. We are receptive, exploratory, and emotionally connected through our right brain first, and then we rely on the emissary of our left brain to symbolize and formalize our understanding through language and logic. We continually check back with the right brain to make sure, like a good musician doing a sound check, that we are hitting the right levels. If need be, we make tweaks and adjustments by consulting with the right brain again—you've seen how some guitarists incorporate tuning even in the midst of a song or slyly between songs—in order to seamlessly make music in a world perpetually ready for new songs.

As therapists, our therapeutic presence is the master, broadly and exquisitely tuning in, and our therapeutic authority is our esteemed emissary, finding the right words at the right time in the right way to reach our clients anew. When these are well integrated, they synergize and continually oscillate to give us the fullest, most three-dimensional moving picture of the client sitting before us.

Mindsight: Integrating the Space Between

Somewhere beyond right and wrong, there
is a garden. I will meet you there.

—Rumi

Despite all of these gifts, of course, being human, we regularly run into problems. The downstairs brain, as Dan Siegel (2010) neatly terms the more foundational brain stem and emotional limbic system, hijacks the upstairs brain—the deliberate, moral, empathic, and measured prefrontal cortex—and doesn't allow us to move forward until we submit to its demands, or at the very least listen to it.

Remember that the downstairs brain is our survivalist animal inheritance powering our most essential tasks, such as breathing, blinking, fighting, and fleeing. It was designed as an exquisitely sensitive danger-alert system and learns very quickly—sometimes, it seems, too quickly—from our emotional experiences to determine who is friend or foe.

Siegel (2010) defines mindsight as a focused attention and grounded equilibrium that allows us to view ourselves and our internal world more clearly so that we don't get swept up in the undertow of our emotional "sea inside" and become slaves to a reactive and limiting mind. Like the neural synapse underlying it, mindsight allows us to create a meditative space that is ripe for creative opportunity and more deeply embodied engagement with ourselves and the world.

Mindsight provides the most powerful tool we have as therapists (and humans) in the sensitive yet essential negotiation between not only the right and left brain but also between the downstairs and upstairs brain too. We constantly complement and yet are at odds with ourselves, and thus it becomes our continuous task through mindsight to work, refine, and finesse that integration.

The rewards of this integration include freedom, flexibility, and compassion on the one hand, and sharpness, resilience, and creative power on the other. And Siegel and others have shown how this operates at both the macro and molecular levels, imbuing us with the kind of equanimity and clarity we need to improvise emotionally and intellectually while simultaneously growing our neural connections throughout the lifespan.

The psyche is built for creative flow and improvisation. Even in dysregulated states, when it is screaming out warning signals to its owner and the world, it is attempting to send out crucial smoke signals for others to emotionally draw near, move back, or shift course.

Lending Mindsight in Therapy

If a man has lost a leg or an eye, he knows he has lost
a leg or an eye; but if he has lost a self—himself—he
cannot know it, because he is no longer there to know it.

—Oliver Sacks, *The Man Who Mistook His*
Wife for a Hat and Other Clinical Tales

It was Freud's great revolution and discovery to notice that the psychological symptoms of distress, many of them neurotic forms of anxiety, depression, and somaticizing, were an attempt at this deeper communication from within or, as he more poetically imagined, from deep in the underground strata of a lost buried city.

Freud also noted how, on a superficial level, these signals, when viewed out of context, appeared "crazy," "degenerate," "immoral," or primitive. We now know them to be nothing of the sort and reclaim them as universal parts of the fantastically complex and difficult task of the noble task of "suffering the slings and arrows of outrageous fortune."

But when things get out of sorts for our patients, it is we who are called in to answer what Schutz (2005) terms the right brain's red phone and help them find themselves again. As Schore (2019) instructs us, we must "implicitly track and resonate with the patterns of rhythmic crescendos/decrescendos of the patient's regulated and dysregulated states of affective arousal."

More simply, we must make new improvisatory music out of the seeming chaos and distortion of the noise of background trauma, and yet we must do so tactfully and in the right brain's own language.

We might think of the right brain's nonverbal and emotionally rich skill as being akin to a national president's crucial role as comforter and consoler-in-chief. We expect the other right brain in the room, especially that of our therapist, to not only tune in but also address the most crucial battles of our current and past experience and to memorialize and integrate them in ways that allow us to be inspired rather than despairing.

We expect our therapists to be largely above the fray and not get entangled too far with us in our enactment or, at the very least, be able to notice and put words to our entanglements so we can become, as relational analyst Anton Hart (2003) says, "usefully entangled." As discussed in "The Case of You" in Chapter 1, an enactment occurs when emotions become so unbearably painful that they can only be communicated indirectly through the unconscious. But rather than just seeing this as something to be scared of, let's lean into the creative possibilities.

What follows are three right-brain tools to help us through. They are geared to help you with some of the most challenging and persnickety clients and situations, the places where improvisation feels most difficult. We'll look at patients who are guarded, those who have suffered massive trauma, and those who are enigmatically intimidating.

Let's get going with some right-brain hacks to help us transform dysregulation, resistance, and overworking into creative improvisation again.

Working the Trifecta: Metaphor, Humor, and Clinical Intuition

BRIDGING OUR TWO HEMISPHERES

Unless you are at home in the metaphor, unless you have had your proper poetical education in the metaphor, you are not safe anywhere.

—Robert Frost (1931)

In Allan Schore's model, metaphor is a central field of interplay between the right and left brain, a place where sharply drawn analytical thinking is connected to dreamlike images. Translating as "carry over," metaphor is a bridge between two worlds. Most of us get an informal education in it, but not the kind Frost is advocating.

Metaphor is fluid, slippery, and dynamic. It readily transforms and sublimates. As Frost said again, "Like a piece of ice on a hot stove, a poem must ride on its own melting" (Barry, 1972). And that applies to metaphor too. It works in a very unique and special way:

All metaphor breaks down somewhere. That is the beauty of it. It is touch and go with the metaphor, and until you have lived with it long enough you don't know when it is going. You don't know how much you can get out of it and when it will cease to yield. It is a very living thing. It is as life itself. (Frost, 1931)

Metaphor shapeshifts before our very eyes but always brings us back to the most eloquent and elemental in our psyches. And we must, as Frost implies, learn the process of seeing how far we can take the metaphor and when a new one is ready to grasp the baton.

A ROYAL AWAKENING

A vibrant and warm 20-something with a kind and reassuring smile that instantly let me know she was in the right field, Amanda came to her first supervision session asking how she could be more comfortable with just being herself in sessions. As if confessing, she said she always considered herself too full of enthusiasm and struggled especially with those guarded patients who gave little back despite her most sincere, thoughtful, and lavish attempts at deep engagement.

It was no wonder. Amanda possessed a vitality that was unmistakable. I riffed with her on that word *enthusiasm*, which literally means to be possessed by the gods, and imagined with her a sort of radiant fire. We toyed with how funny it was that her very sunshine could be seen as a bad thing and something to hold back, and as we investigated, she noted how quickly she fell into the role of helping others to find their own words, their own sunshine.

It was easy to see how natural and foundational this quality was to her, an essential part of her identity and very constitution. And as we talked further, we also noted how it was also informed by nurture, how at a very young age she was tasked with mediating her parent's divorce for her much younger sister. We sourced how important it was for her to maintain the flame of her sister and by extension a younger part of herself and, in so doing, protect a cherished and beautiful form of innocence.

We even began to notice the shadow side of this light, how especially with resistant and reluctant patients, she felt like she was doing all of the work. We tracked how she felt resentful—though she was too kind to admit it—for having to work so much harder, and being out on a limb with her heart on her sleeve while the patient sat comfortably rejecting her offerings with silence or one-word answers. There was a side of her that felt angry to have to do this work again with patients as she did unconsciously as a child.

But she felt guilty too. She thought she should slow things down and give others more space to get there themselves. It was as if she was being selfish.

As we talked, the metaphor shifted for me, and I switched from an emotional metaphor to an intellectual one, albeit turning it on its head. That's what metaphor does too. It engages us in a paradox of divergent and convergent thinking, allowing us to see new angles and aspects of what is familiar while simultaneously playing with its very strangeness.

"You know, Amanda, I think your enthusiasm is actually fantastic, but it's more like you see like a chessmaster, 10 to 15 moves ahead. We don't want to stop that at all. We want to connect with that more fully!"

Intrigued and puzzled, she leaned in, as if to say, "Keep talking." It was her turn now to wait for more from the other side.

"Yeah, but this chess game is different. It isn't adversarial. You've always been ready to help figure out the moves others could make so you could reach their kingdom and castles, not so you could attack them. You're happy to share the wealth of your kingdom with them too."

Her eyebrows arched as if to say, "So this is a *good* thing?"

"Yes, it's such a gift to be able to see so many moves ahead, and it's so healthy for you to see that with pride, just as we've done with this word *enthusiasm*. Possessed by the gods—you are royalty!"

At the same time, I was also illuminating her inner conflict. It would be too fast and too aggressive for her, especially as a child, to tell her parents she wished they had thought more moves ahead and had maintained the healthy kingdom where the queen and king live side by side, flanked and protected by a court of noble knights, bishops, and foot soldiers.

In contrast to her guarded clients, she had to suppress the adversarial side of herself and overcompensate for it with her thoughtful sunshine. As we talked however, we could reappropriate this adversarial side—as echoed in the chess image— and see its connection to a completely different model, one that moved outside the petty constraints of a zero-sum game.

We also saw that this metaphor could be a gift and new offering to her guarded clients too. So many of them saw intimacy as an implicit chess game, one to be rightfully wary and strategic about. How might their vibrant new therapist possibly force them out from their corners and expose the vulnerability of that famous divine couple in all of us? Wouldn't it be a surprise for them too to learn that instead of a war, the objective of this new metaphorical game was the opposite, to get as close as possible to each other's royal courts?

For both Amanda and myself, as well as her clients, we could find and discover together that new metaphors change the very architecture of thought and feeling itself. Operating from the inside out, metaphors do this in a most gentle and potent way, naturally forming the kind of right and left integration that is at the heart of feeling fully alive.

HUMOR ME FOR A MOMENT

Paulina had been through hundreds of therapists. She was currently working with a separate therapist for her cognitive-behavioral work to relieve anxiety, depression, and perfectionism, and a relational therapist—my supervisee—to dig deep into the source of her relational trauma and glimmering desire for more fulfilling romantic relationships and greater authenticity.

This strategy showcased her incipient hope for change and possibility and the underlying terror of being fully owned in any one relationship that could take away her power. A confusing but so very human blend, it was not surprising to witness her consistently blunt and sarcastic resistance of her therapist's agenda at every turn. "This strategy won't work with me. If you say or do that—sound needy or act too pushy—I will leave this therapy too."

Paulina had sporadic contact with a narcissistic mother and absent father, who both left her, like many Eastern European children of the fast-crumbling communist era, in the care of her lukewarm but emotionally underintelligent grandparents. She found great success in her career as a tech innovator and was known for her quick and sharp wit, but she constantly found herself connecting in her personal life to what she felt were the most damaged "undesirables," as she liked to call them. Other victims of abandonment, emotional trauma, and neglect, she hated being part of their club. At her core, she felt unlovable, a black hole of self-disgust with only an agile mind and Cheshire Cat grin to protect her.

As I listened to my supervisee John talk about her, I could sense his frustration at her unwillingness to seriously engage his overtures for positive growth. On this day, he was both lamenting and resisting her subversive disinterest in trying out a new word of the year, an affirmation, challenge, and mantra rolled into one that all clinicians in the practice were sharing with their patients to ring in January's arrival.

John took it as his opportunity to get past Paulina's defenses and to help her—once and for all!—orient, affirm, and work toward a newfound understanding of herself. Around the edges of John's youthful idealism—he was just shy of 30—and well-meaning optimism, though, I could sense a vexed and subtly critical jab, as if to say, "I prepare for you this five-course meal of only hope and possibility, and all you can do is snub it with a sarcastic request for a McDonald's Happy Meal!" (cf. Bromberg, 2006).

Again I could imagine Paulina's Cheshire Cat grin. I fantasized the effect it would have if John had actually said this to her. Paulina would delight in the irony and wit of herself as communist-era transplant begging for capitalism's most popular trashy meal. "If you must force me to be American trash too, I will reappropriate it in my own mordant, Romanian way."

I struggled with how to tell John about my own right-brained reverie, awash in metaphor but also steeped in its own humor. In contrast to Paulina's humor, which veered between an acerbic trickster and a defensive viper, I wanted a humor that was undeniably playful, open, and creative.

"I see why you are so bothered and troubled by Paulina's behavior in sessions, her lack of gratitude for both your efforts and for your method. And I also see why she is so resistant to you. You want to rescue the princess, but she wants you to slay the dragon first. You both have very good reasons to be unhappy." I offered this as an out to the dilemma before both of them, using humor conjoined with metaphor as greater permission to engage the intensifying pull arising from their mutual tug of war.

Liberated from a sort of shame, John confessed his concerns about being another traumatizing perpetrator to Paulina, and his own mixed feelings around taking on his own authority without becoming a brute. This connected to his greater comfort with therapeutic presence as compared to therapeutic authority, and the anxiety and stress he was feeling at the challenge she was unconsciously throwing at him.

I told him that the best news was this patient would provide a creative opportunity for him to integrate these issues more fully, and that he in turn, by engaging, mirroring, and modeling the inner dialogue of this process, would help the patient creatively transcend the limited narratives of her past as well.

I instructed him to lean in more to the playful use of metaphor and humor with her to mirror her very clear capacities there and to model for her a new, related way of talking about the painful and difficult things as well as the hopeful and good things that had heretofore felt unattainable, shameful, and distant in a sour grapes kind of way. I told John that this could help these moments be better digested by all.

He got my pun, and was able to smile rather than slink away from this new creative opportunity.

MOBILIZING YOUR CLINICAL INTUITION

Like a biological instinct, clinical intuition is a gut-driven, right-brain capacity to quickly size up and express what you are seeing in the moment and to do so with such accuracy that it feels uncanny. Malcolm Gladwell (2005) rhapsodized its many varieties in his popular book *Blink*, showcasing the capacity for couples researcher John Gottman (Gottman & Silver, 1999) to predict with near 90% accuracy if a couple was doomed for divorce after watching only about 5 minutes of video footage or the famous art conservator who instantly differentiated between the real McCoy and the sculptural stunt double.

Nick came into session each week shaking my hand firmly, and as we walked up the creaking, carpeted stairs of the

Victorian cottage that housed the university counseling center, he asked how I was doing like he was in his 40s with two kids of his own, just consulting another peer. Already a superstar in the art world, he would plop down onto the chair facing me in his geek-chic glasses and cross his legs to display his signature mismatched socks.

I wasn't much older than Nick at the time, just slightly north of my 30s as he was of his 20s. His approach bemused, confused, and rankled me in ways I couldn't quite put into words. Why did it so often feel like he was the parent and I was the child, or, worse yet, why did I sometimes feel like he was patronizing me through his unusually warm salutations?

After a session or two, I decided to trust my clinical intuition and ask him about it, rather than continue to fret. There was something that seemed important about it. As they say, if it was wrong to talk about it, I didn't want to be right. And yet comically enough, it was the right brain itself that was spurring my confidence to take the plunge.

"Nick, I noticed something that I wanted to ask you about. I could be totally wrong, but sometimes when we say hello at the beginning of a session, I can't help but feel like you're a used car salesman convincing me to buy a car I didn't know I needed. I don't know why and I was wondering if you can help me figure it out."

He lit up, nearly elated that I picked up something in him that hardly anybody ever so warmly called him on. "I'm so glad you noticed. My father always taught me how to 'kill 'em with kindness,' and it's something that I just can't stop doing no matter how hard I try. Nobody ever dares to say anything about it because I'm so good at it. Wow, I can't believe you got that!"

Because I had braced for him to take major offense, I was surprised too. In my mind, I was already prepping to soften my statement in case he became so hurt and angry that our rapport started to nosedive. But by trusting and leaning into my clinical intuition, something very profound and authentic began to unfold.

Again, notice how I wrapped together a metaphor with playful humor and served it hot from the clinical intuition that prompted it. His positive response goaded me on and unleashed another image I couldn't stop seeing in my head.

"Nick, I don't know why, but I just keep seeing this image of a character from a movie and I want to share it with you to see if it means anything. There's this Wes Anderson film called *Rushmore*, and the main character is a very intellectual, artistic, and precocious high school student who somehow reminds me of you."

"Oh my god, that's my favorite film. Max Fischer was my hero in high school!"

Clinical intuition is uncanny, and yet, it is also just part of how we are built. The right brain knows how to listen for what is underground and like a seismograph can detect even the slightest rumblings and shifts.

President of the beekeeping, fencing, and acting clubs, and a host of other offbeat attractions, Max is an eccentric high school student at the elite private school Rushmore Academy, and he is obsessed with winning the love of Miss Cross, an adorably shy British first grade teacher who herself is a precociously young widower.

Like Nick, Max is smart beyond his years and also struggles with neurotic insecurities in romantic relationships that he deflects with his intellect and charm. He too knows expertly how to kill with kindness.

In a pivotally telling scene, Max sits across from Miss Cross at the library and magically anticipates her every need and desire as she grades papers. Just as her glass is emptied, he fills it with lemonade, and then as her pen fades, he immediately readies another one as its replacement, casually discarding the old one with a maestro's flourish. Max portrays the confident omnipotence of a man and yet, with his Clark Kent glasses and prep school tie, it is clear that he is really just a boy.

"Has it ever crossed your mind that you're far too young for me?" Miss Cross gently yet sharply implores, one step away from losing patience, like I almost did with Nick. You can see her trying earnestly to protect his tender feelings yet bristling at being both patronized and seduced at the same time.

As she presses on to remind him of his place—she is a teacher and he is a student—Max passive–aggressively sharpens a pencil in a childish attempt to reassert his control and position in the face of what can only feel inside like a heartbreaking rejection. On the surface, though, Max smooth-talks her in the persona of a peer, saying glibly, "The truth is, neither one of us have the slightest idea where this relationship is going. We can't predict the future."

Miss Cross holds steady in maintaining the boundary between them, reasserting the truth that there is no relationship other than a friendship since he is just 15 years old. By making a compromise on wording to spare his feelings and holding firm on her role as the authority rather than as a peer, Miss Cross, like me with Nick, challenges Max to go deeper into his feelings and stop killing with kindness.

In a soft, higher-pitched voice, he tenderly and vulnerably acknowledges that he has never met anyone like Miss Cross and, in the glimmer of a moment, we see the boy inside as much as out, finally up close and personal.

With cheeks almost flushed, as if blushing on his behalf, Miss Cross echoes his singsong voice and responds kindly and gingerly, letting the tempo of her initial irritation peter out into a moment of understated tenderness: "I think I can safely say I've never met anyone like you either."

"You haven't, have you?" he says in that aw-shucks way that only a man looking to be seen in his gooey center can muster. And then, soon enough, he's back to his old tricks again in that precocious, pretentious mix of insecurity and charm for which Wes Andersen is so famous.

"Want to shake hands?"

And the camera pulls back on the awkwardly sweet and jarringly funny moment of seeing Max, nearly a foot shorter, reaching out his hand like a man yet looking so undeniably boyish again.

Uncanny yes, but the clinical intuition that led to this connection was elaborately accurate and amazingly prescient of the work that was to follow. In only our second session, by trusting my intuition and calling forth this scene, I was able to have a full handle on the unique and intriguing mix of slick insecurity, warm pretentiousness, and endearingly off-putting charm that Nick presented and we would soon unpack.

WHY WE NEED THE RIGHT-BRAIN TRIFECTA

It's crucial to remember that using metaphor, humor, and clinical intuition isn't just for our patients. They are just as much for us in staying integrated, regulated, fluid, and free in sessions too. In fact, I consider them to be the crucial air we need to prevent our metaphorical tires from going flat, what others more conventionally note as the experience of burning out.

This whole therapy business is one of the most unique and unusual jobs because we are using ourselves as the instrument and vehicle of change. It's why we constantly need to make sure, as mindfulness expert Jon Kabat-Zinn (2019) notes, that like the New York Philharmonic, we are well tuned before we play. And let me take it one step even further. We constantly need to make adjustments mid-performance so that we are proud and confident in the music we are making together. We owe it to ourselves and our patients to consistently right the left brain so that our improvisations create new moments of art for our patients and ourselves.

In the next section, we'll talk briefly about some other self-care strategies for making sure we keep creatively and sustainably focused as clinicians.

Emotional Sustainability as a New Clinician

As therapists, we are often so intrigued by nurture—after all, it's our primary area of focus and leverage—that it's easy for us to forget nature. Jerome Kagan's (Kagan & Snidman, 2004) extraordinary body of research highlights this ironic fact. So it should come as no surprise that we also forget nature for the most important person in the room: ourselves.

There are four different aspects of temperament and personality we should know if we want to practice therapy in a compassionate, fulfilling, and sustainable manner, one that supports our newfound whole-brain integration.

While we might have learned about these concepts in undergrad or graduate school, odds are pretty high that most have not focused on how important they are for maintaining and depleting your energy, and keeping you in the sweet spot needed for your professional and personal well-being as a therapist.

If we were to analogize ourselves to cars, there are basically four varieties: gas-powered, electric-powered, hybrids, and race cars. The gas-powered among us are the extroverts, the people most energized and fueled by social engagement, the aficionados of schmoozing at cocktail parties, yucking it up at large group outings, and moving in and out as social butterflies among a variety of people. These folks are the ones who are best oriented to and excited by what is happening from the outside in and thrive on reaching high enough levels of emotional stimulation to feel worth the price of admission.

Too much alone time makes their skin crawl and leaves them restless for the adrenaline rush of the vibrant, social world. Their strongest suit, however, is their capacity to take risks, putting themselves out there, marketing themselves, and initiating with confidence in ways that make them natural leaders. Not surprisingly, as Susan Cain (2013), author of *Quiet*, notes, since the publication of the first American self-help book, *How to Win Friends and Influence People* by Dale Carnegie in 1936, extroverts have been the gold standard of leadership and wellness in America. While there are probably too many to name, notable extroverts include Steve Jobs, Bill Clinton, Dolly Parton, Franklin Roosevelt, Martin Luther King Jr., and Paul McCartney.

The electric-powered, in contrast, the introverts, are charged up by either their own treasured solitude, one-on-one in-depth conversations with their significant other or best friend, or limited dosages of socializing that leave them with enough time to recoup at their home charging station, a good book, or documentary.

These people are most oriented to, stimulated by, and intrigued with what is happening internally, under the surface, and in the depths. They are deliberate, reflective, and quiet. They hate small talk and would find nothing better than if people would just eliminate it and get to the good stuff. Spending too much time at parties and at the mercy of an overly external world knocks the stuffing out of them. Notable introverts include Eleanor Roosevelt, Rosa Parks, Gandhi, Steve Wozniak, Michael Jordan, George Harrison, and Hillary Clinton.

The hybrids are a variety not much discussed and are often confused for each of the former. Both introverted and extroverted, the ambiverts have a unique and seemingly contradictory capacity to be highly gregarious and solitary at alternate moments. They get their energy from both deep inward reflection and highly engaging social connection. In fact, they are the most happy and energized when they are fully and equally fueled and charged up. Notable exemplars here include Abraham Lincoln, Oprah Winfrey, Fred Rogers, Roger Federer, Barack Obama, Sonia Sotomayor, Stephen Colbert, Duke Ellington, and Kendrick Lamar.

Ambiverts have a gift, a capacity to profoundly empathize with those around them—to tune in to others' deepest hopes and fears while simultaneously staying connected to their own. Research by organizational psychologist Adam Grant (2013) backs up this claim of an ambivert superpower, an emotional depth perception he calls the ambivert advantage.

In a surprising study, he found that extroverts were not the best salespeople, as had long been touted. Instead, the often-sidelined ambiverts, because of their capacity to perceptively notice and respond to the social environment and genuinely express their own inner experience, were much better at making and closing deals. In other words, because they are naturally and instinctively well versed in their introverted and extroverted selves, they bridge the gap between inner and outer experience and draw on the best of both worlds.

The last group, the race cars, might seem unexpected. They are the highly sensitive people (Aron, 1996), the HSPs, and I call them race cars because they take the turns so fast and are such responsive vehicles that they need to get to the pit to change their tires and oil very frequently. Neurologically built to perceive and process with great depth what they are picking up in their environment—sound, light, emotion, and everything in between—like the introverts and ambiverts, they too can easily get drained and burned out from too much stimulation. (In fact, there are some who wonder if ambiverts are a special combination better known as highly sensitive extroverts.) Either way, HSPs are very adept at quickly and deeply processing people and the environment.

Maintaining Your Energy

What impact does this have on you? It's critical for you to know which group or groups you fall into so you can make sure you are maintaining the proper energy and noticing when you are at very low fuel or battery.

Extroverts are well advised to make sure they get enough stimulation outside of session (unless they are running groups!), an engaging social life at home and at work, and also a healthy dose of tempering self-reflection to balance out their highly external natures.

For the HSPs, introverts, and ambiverts, it is crucial to know when you are getting overstimulated and need proper recharging. Think of it like knowing when your emotional cell phone battery is getting to 5 or 10% or like you are about to get hangry soon. Too much stimulation in back-to-back sessions, long and drawn-out group meetings, an overscheduled social calendar, or little time for refilling the well alone can leave the HSP, introvert, or ambivert frazzled, crabby, and relatively useless. Not to worry: their keen focus, perceptive engagement, and high energy will perk right up with the right amount and quality of down time.

It is also helpful for introverts, ambiverts, and HSPs to make sure they set up their offices in such a way as to protect their sensibilities, including dimmer lighting, freedom from too much distracting noise, and regular opportunities for creative outlets to download the tremendous residue that the taxing work of therapy can bring on. I would often take regular lunch breaks practicing piano in a quiet practice room, walk outside in nature away from the busy college counseling center, or stagger my schedule so I could get a much-needed break and recharge from the busy emotional work of psychotherapy.

It is very likely that these distinctions in temperament start early, as Jerome Kagan has chronicled. Researchers (Boyce, 2019) have forwarded another useful metaphor to make this taxonomy easy to spot and self-diagnose. "Dandelions" refer to the majority of children who show a biological indifference to experiences of stress and adversity, thriving in almost any environment. "Orchids" are the minority of children—about one in five—that show an extraordinary susceptibility to both negative and positive social contexts, showing very high sensitivity and stress responses to adversity. "Tulips" fall somewhere in between, showing both a sensitivity and resilience not seen in either group.

Just as we are going to be tending to the nature and nurture of our patients, we must do so for ourselves and recognize how we are built. As so many of the more experienced clinicians tell us, this helps us maintain a sustainable practice.

Right Brain Rising

The right brain has ascended so fast these days because of economic and cultural trends, as noted in Daniel Pink's (2009) trailblazing book *A Whole New Mind: Why Right-Brainers Will Rule the Future.* As a result of the three As—abundance, Asia, and automation—aesthetics and meaning, the central province of the right brain, are not only essential, but in the highest demand ever.

Automation means that people need to add value beyond

what computers and left-brained thinking alone can do. The Asia part of the equation reminds us that cheap and ubiquitous outsourcing demands that we be more than just technicians. Instead, we must develop meaningful and personally tailored relationships, a capacity to decipher novel solutions, and the skill to synthesize it all with the big picture in full view.

As Pink notes: "In an age of abundance, appealing only to rational, logical and functional needs is woefully insufficient. Engineers must figure out how to get things to work. But if those things are not pleasing to the eye or compelling to the soul, few will buy them" (p. 34). Or, as he comically puts it, "When I'm on my deathbed, it's unlikely that I'll look back on my life and say, 'Well, I've made some mistakes. But at least I snagged one of those Michael Graves toilet brushes back in 2004'" (p. 35).

EXERCISE 1: Working the Trifecta

METAPHOR MAKING

How do we tap into metaphor? We allow ourselves to let an image and thought come together—like when we are squinting our eyes at those old Magic Eye pictures—and something emerges. It's helpful to allow a metaphor to come from some completely different domain and to court the irreverent—it's the right brain talking here. Remember my client as a used-car salesman?

Eventually you might even develop a useful menu of metaphors to use in different situations. To discuss anxiety or trauma, I've used metaphors of an undertow, quicksand, kryptonite, a spinning compass, treading water while holding a boulder, and any other imaginative comparison of this—anxiety—to that, i.e., insert metaphorical image here.

What metaphors do you find helpful in describing anxiety, depression, or any other clinical disorder that is worth metaphorizing?

Metaphor also becomes your barometer—ooh, a meta-metaphor!—for how much you are connecting and engaging your right brain in your sessions. As one patient used to tell me, "I know how present and connected you are by how many metaphors you use in the session." He'd playfully jibe at me: "Mike, it's already been 15 minutes and I haven't heard a good metaphor yet!"

Remember that metaphor is also a very safe place for us and our clients to talk about what is difficult to discuss. And like play for children, it engages us in the symbol rather than talking about it directly through explicit left-brain analysis. It plays first and explains second.

As Robert Frost says of poetry, metaphor "provides the one permissible way of saying one thing and meaning another" (Barry, 1972). Isn't it nice to know that our statements to clients can be forms of poetry? That's what they are looking for to heal and grow, and it is also what makes our work so rewarding and fulfilling too.

So court, practice, and share metaphor widely and freely with your clients. You'll be helping them to make the right-brain connection that heals trauma and opens creativity and connection, and you'll also be freeing yourself to enjoy the beauty and reap the psychic income that comes so regularly from our work.

HUMOR

Humor is a way for us to engage the trickster, the side of self that loves to talk about what is on the edge. It's subversive and creative, but it can also be close to aggression and defensiveness, so we have to treat humor like fire. Make sure it is harnessed and that there's a curtain on the fireplace so the flames or embers don't burn anybody up.

It is especially important for us to use and model how to inject humor playfully both in our tone and in our timing. The most effective and creative humor reduces shame, gives more permission to explore and emote, and opens up a space for new dialogue together (Wachtel, 1993). Even that used-car salesman metaphor was delivered in a humorous way with the tag "I didn't even know I needed this car!" so that it could be explored more safely.

Be mindful of your client's capacity for humor and how they use it too.

- Do they resort to barbs, jabs, or digs at others or self?
- Does their humor playfully express the ambivalences and conflicts that they are currently challenged to sort through?
- Is there an evolution in the way they are using humor over time, moving from sarcasm to playfulness?

Again, this is another barometer for how the client is doing, how you are doing, and how the relationship is going. Use it much, but use it wisely.

CLINICAL INTUITION

Clinical intuition is the "Spidey sense" we have as clinicians about a feeling, thought, or pattern that we are picking up that's very much in the room. Like mindsight (Siegel, 2010) itself, it's a seventh sense.

Many new clinicians are worried about imposing their clinical intuition or being wrong. It's okay. Your clinical intuition can stay internal as you test out if there's any data to support it, or it can be shared sensitively with your client.

I tell my patients from the start of therapy, "Sometimes I'm going to try out something enthusiastically, but I want you to tell me if it's really on target, totally off-base, or something in between. You are the ultimate authority on it, and I'm working for you."

When unsure if your clinical intuition is right, you can always soften it: "This might be totally off, but I'm getting a sense that . . . "; "I don't know if this is barking up the right tree or not, but I keep having this image or feeling and I'm wondering if you can help me make sense of it"; "This may be nothing, but I keep wondering about this. . . . "

Again, engage the client in joining the exploration with you and model for them that it's okay to be wrong and even to not know. They will appreciate your imperfection—and likely be better able to bear their own too as a result—and your authentic willingness to take risks to get to know them better.

Ultimately, your clinical intuition becomes another right-brain tool to help you hone in on the therapeutic authority we'll talk about in Chapter 6. It's like singing from your diaphragm with your therapeutic voice—like an opera singer, you'll be able to sing anything and project anywhere as a result of tapping into this force.

EXERCISE 2: Maintaining Your Energy and a Sustainable Practice

There are both formal and informal tests to determine whether you are an introvert, extrovert, ambivert, or HSP. I recommend Susan Cain's website for the introvert/extrovert distinction (https://www.quietrev.com/the-introvert-test/) and Daniel

Pink's ambivert assessment on his website (https://www.danpink .com/assessment/). Elaine Aron also has a simple self-report survey to determine if you are an HSP (https://hsperson.com/test/ highly-sensitive-test/). Use these pieces of information to learn your dominant and foundational way of getting energy so you can more easily maintain your sweet spot personally and professionally, and so you can begin to build a sustainable and fulfilling practice.

2

WEAVING TOGETHER MANY VOICES: THERAPEUTIC POLYPHONY

What do a 13th-century Persian Sufi mystic poet, 16th-century English playwright, 18th-century German composer, 19th-century gay American poet, 20th-century English proto-feminist novelist, 20th-century Chilean communist diplomat, and 21st-century poet all have in common?

No, this isn't a setup for a joke.

All of these diverse figures across history—Jalal Rumi, William Shakespeare, Johann Sebastian Bach, Walt Whitman, Virginia Woolf, Pablo Neruda, and Tony Hoagland—discovered and forwarded a vision of the human psyche as a collection of conflicting, collaborative, and maddeningly fascinating multiple selves. These multiple selves provide the basic structures out of which all of the seemingly invisible changes of our therapeutic improvisation occur. They are the constantly shifting chords and stories out of which a dynamic life is built, but yet they can also be terribly difficult to work with in life and in therapy (Bromberg, 2006/2011; Rubin, 2011; Stern, 2009).

A Polyphonic Mind and Heart

Johann Sebastian Bach, the master baroque composer, introduced us to the intricate and complex beauty of these constantly fleeing voices and ushered in music's beginnings as a polyphonic art. Bach showcased that while we start with one voice and melody, it is not soon enough before another starts itching to get into the game too. And before too long there are four or five voices competing and weaving in and out, all the while gracing us with unexpectedly beautiful harmonic changes in their wake.

Not surprisingly, these pieces are called fugues because it feels like the lines are chasing and fleeing each other. If you listen to one of the masters of the Bach fugue—Glenn Gould—you can hear the strange beauty of trying to hold together the many and the one, and in so doing, transcending them all. This is the essence of multiplicity.

As in music, we are built first with a polyphonic mind and heart—a number of inner voices scrambling for attention—and only later do we learn how to tame them and make monophonic music that features a steadily accompanied and virtuosic solo line. As we get more sophisticated, we integrate the two—the polyphonic and monophonic—and learn how to separate each line, when it needs to solo and when it needs to pull back and just accompany. And even better, on our best days, the line between the two is so seamless that hardly any of us can tell which kind of music we are truly making.

Multiplicity From the Inside Out

For a simpler, more visual representation of multiplicity, let's look at the 2015 Disney Pixar movie *Inside Out* (Doctor & Del Carmen, 2015), where we find each emotion—fear, sadness, joy, disgust, and anger—embodied in different characters all crowded around psychic mission control in a girl named Riley. Each character, at one point or another, steps up to take the controls and jockeys for position to shape our protagonist's moment-to-moment destiny, just as we all do in wrestling with our quite unruly multiplicity.

In one scene, Riley has just moved cross-country with her family, and she is showing signs of the tween angst of sadness, confusion, and not-belonging that is so hard to put into words. Her attuned mother catches this at the dinner table and attempts to signal her to open up while simultaneously cueing her husband.

We see inside each of their minds this committee of selves fighting and the cacophony that ensues because they are all out of sync. Riley is moving quickly between her angry, fearful, and disgusted selves and takes little comfort and consolation from her mother's kind desire to tap into her sadness. Riley doesn't want to touch that with a 39-and-a-half-foot pole.

Her father, disrupted from watching a hockey match inside his own head, leans in on his angry and fearful selves to control the situation rather than investigate. The disgusted and angry selves in Riley push her father to unleash his "def-con two" strategy of "putting down the foot," censuring her for her attitude and unceremoniously and uncharacteristically sending her to her room. By the end of the sequence, everyone is dysregulated, and Riley bellows, as if to cadence it all, "Just shut up!!"

The multiple sides of self that usually work together—inside and between the characters—are at cross purposes. Even worse, the side that can't be talked about—the profound sadness at losing one's home and sense of meaning—are avoided at all costs. "Just shut up!" Riley is telling both them and herself, and as a result of this falling under the radar, everyone gets caught in a spiral of rage and disintegration.

The Discovery of Multiplicity in Literature

Writers Hoagland, Neruda, Rumi, Whitman, and Woolf noted the disruptiveness of these sides too. Rumi envisioned these selves like unexpected and unwelcome guests, ready to rummage through your house, bringing shame, malice, depression, and meanness. And yet he instructs us to greet them wholeheartedly and even laugh, for these sides will "clear you out for some new delight" and function as a "guide from beyond" (Rumi & Washington, 2006).

Relational analyst Philip Bromberg (2006) keenly notes multiplicity's discovery by modernist novelist Virginia Woolf. Wisely yet understatedly, she observes,

> these selves of which we are built up, one on top of another, as plates are piled on a waiter's hand, have . . . little constitutions and rights of their own.
>
> One will only come if it is raining, another [will emerge only] in a room with green curtains, another when Mrs. Jones is not there, another if you can promise it a glass of wine—and so on. . . . Everybody can multiply from his own experience the different terms which his different selves have made with him—and some are too wildly ridiculous to be mentioned in print at all. (pp. 308–309)

Our multiplicity is unruly. In his poem "We Are Many," Pablo Neruda (2015) confesses, "Of the many men whom I am, whom we are, I cannot settle on a single one." His cowardly self arrives when his brave self is desired, and an arsonist appears on scene when a firefighter is needed. He is so lost that he never knows who he is or who he will next become. Wondering if he is alone in this predicament, suffering some strange and cruel fate, he dreams of ringing a bell to call forth his most essential self, so that he never slips away. He wonders if others wrestle and reckon with the dilemmas of this slippery existence too.

So thoroughly intrigued and puzzled by the wild discrepancies of our inner selves, Neruda's speaker decides that instead of trying to locate or explain himself and his problems, in the future he will only find himself properly by speaking in terms of geography. Our states of self are so vast and wide that this is the only lexicon that can truly encompass us.

Poet Tony Hoagland introduces us to multiplicity through a Neruda-esque man raking leaves. Mindlessly humming Madonna's "Like a Virgin," a song he could swear he actually hates, it dawns on him that the head and heart are in such different time zones that they only allow us to find out tomorrow what we actually feel today.

How curiously the self is built, how funny that it operates in a perpetual state of jet lag. What a strange capacity we all have to move back and forth between a maddening variety of self-states, including that earworm we didn't realize was still with us.

Hoagland's speaker enjoys the beauty and order of the gleaming red and orange piles of leaves but doesn't understand the leaf removal process, identifying so much more with the entropy of the wind. He feels more at home in the seeming disorder of randomness, yet it perturbs and puzzles him that it should feel second nature to be so scattered.

Pondering further, he arrives at alarming examples of his own fragmentation, our very powerful and human capacity for dissociation, fantasizing about a TV program while looking at the sky and imagining the book he means to read while attending a dinner party.

This constantly shifting multiplicity becomes so disconcerting that he almost concludes that he is never really anywhere. Ready to give up his own pride and purpose, he laments his—and by extension the whole of humanity's—perpetual dislocation.

Lucky for us, Hoagland rescues his speaker with the consolation that multiplicity is the core of what makes him and us fully human. Referencing the sciences and the arts through Darwin and Keats, he reminds us that this capacity for division is also at the heart of the capacity for creation. Both of them could discover something revolutionary while temporarily being somewhere else, playing poker, or doing surgery.

It is the paradoxical propensity to be both "lost and found" that we find in life that gives it the ring of joy and hope, even in the seemingly most disconnected moments. It allows us to glide in and out of a diversity of emotional spaces and gives us a sense of depth and breadth. And as Hoagland concludes, it is in this place where we can have the "strange conviction" that we are going to be born.

The crescendo of this vision comes in none other than the colossus himself, Walt Whitman. In "Song of Myself," Whitman (1997) celebrates and proclaims the wonder and beauty of our multiplicity in his revolutionary free verse: "Do I contradict myself? Very well then, I contradict myself, I am large, I contain multitudes."

And it is to this, the containing and expressing of these multitudes, in ourselves and our work as therapists, to which I now turn.

Multiplicity Defined

Multiplicity is the fundamental operating system of the psyche and what unites the unconscious and conscious that Freud discovered and brought together in a model of the mind and brain. It incorporates our capacity to dissociate, shift, and transport among a variety of different self-states, narratives, or, as I like to think of it, different possible chord changes. It's no wonder we have to learn how to improvise so well as therapists.

Bromberg notes,

> A flexible relationship among self-states through the use
> of ordinary dissociation is what allows a human being to
> engage the ever-shifting requirements of life's complexities
> with creativity and spontaneity. It is what gives a person
> the remarkable capacity to negotiate character and
> change simultaneously—to stay the same while changing.
> (2016, p. 2)

We all have multiple selves, held together in a dynamic interplay based on the context of inner and outer circumstances (Bromberg, 2006). Diagnostically speaking, it is nearly impossible to get a sense for what is normal and adaptive for a client unless you know the unique context in which they took shape (Mitchell, 1988). The contextual nature of self is analogous to the use of color in Mark Rothko's abstract paintings; the color can only be truly understood and experienced in relation to the hue next to it. Similarly, it is crucial to get to know the relational matrix out of which your client has formed in order to accurately understand the color of their experience and how it may be reworked in the presence of new possibilities.

In order to better understand how multiplicity functions, we need another handy metaphor. As in the movie *Inside Out*, therapy brings all of the different selves to the metaphorical table so that we can have a conversation. Some selves will talk more, some less, and others might not even be invited or allowed at the table at all. This last category is the most interesting and disruptive, as it consists of not-me, the part of self that has been so thoroughly hurt, shamed, or neglected that it is virtually inexpressible and unimaginable (Bromberg, 2006; Stern, 2009). Discerning and identifying which side of self is speaking at the table is crucial for treatment, as is recognizing the relative airtime each side of self has had in the client's larger life story.

Finding Good-Me and Bad-Me

It's relatively simple and straightforward to conjure up good-me or bad-me sides in therapy. Most people are happy to talk about the aspects of themselves they are proud of and value deeply. Whether it is being generous, hardworking, resourceful, smart, funny, successful, or any other aspect, these qualities are harmonically consonant and pleasing, and it is as easy to bring them out as for a conductor to call on the violins to bring out the main melody. In fact, it is common for many strength-based therapists to do just this, lean in on this section of the psyche to help bolster the sides that typically bring out more dissonance and conflict.

Bad-me sides are also not so difficult to bring out, if we do it in a permissive and self-respecting way (Wachtel, 1993). In fact, bringing out aspects of self that people do not like, their jealousy, resentment, anger, sadness, or any other facet that they have been socialized into judging, is the point of therapy itself: illuminating the hidden conflicts that give rise to the anxiety, depression, and general discontent and unhappiness that brings people into our offices in the first place (Watchtel, 1993).

We can think of bad-me as the necessary dissonance that gives our psychological music its tension, its interest, and its motivation for some next, new, pleasing or restful cadence. Without bad-me, we ourselves wouldn't be an interesting or dynamic character to follow at all; we'd be inert and would have few chemical reactions in ourselves or in our relationships.

Working With Not-Me and Enactments

Not-me is the hinge from which either a mutual devolution or creative inspiration can occur. When it devolves, it can become a polarizing, marginalizing, and mutually traumatizing force, and yet when it opens, it can become the most authentic, connecting, fulfilling, and holistic experience imaginable.

Not-me parts of self find their way into the therapeutic dialogue in the form of enactments, whereby parts of the dissociated and split-off feelings and thoughts get shared by therapist and patient, each holding it together in an unformulated way, like two broken halves of a plate (Stern, 2009). This is initially experienced as something that both patient and therapist ward off in a hot-potato fashion, such that the other person is initially to blame for the feelings and thoughts that seem to intrude.

Stern says that enactments are our clients' attempts at putting into interpersonal form what they must dissociate for psychic survival. Although on the surface they seem like disruptive and destructive elements, they are poignant and hopeful right-brain attempts to reach out to the therapist's capacity to transform nonverbal right-brain pleas into new creative relational forms. In other words, they form the beating heart and soul of therapeutic improvisation.

With greater reflection and emotional receptivity, the therapist brings shape to not-me experience by transforming it into something about the interpersonal situation or even by sharing his or her not-me identification. This polyphony is tricky, but with practice, we get more skilled with easing the not-me melodic line back into the music.

In the introduction, we saw the not-me of Matt Damon's character in *Good Will Hunting*, the psychological places that, like Harry Potter's Voldemort (Rowling, 1999), cannot and will not be named and the persistently aggressive yet poignant attempts at keeping his therapist away from the places of hurt, vulnerability, and pain that resulted from being the victim of physical and emotional abuse at the hands of his father. These moments culminated in Robin Williams's iconic moment of therapist comfort after sensitively sharing the naming of his own not-me abuse: "It's not your fault, Will."

We also saw Dwayne in *Little Miss Sunshine* fighting with everything in his fiber to keep away the not-me feeling of being a total loser—just like everybody else in his eccentric but dysfunctional family—and instead wanting to literally and metaphorically soar above it all.

In Chapter 1's "A Case of You," we witnessed the not-me of a first-year student struggling against me as therapist and yet trying desperately to communicate through our relationship. Without a right-brain-driven trust in the signals of nonverbal pain and an intuitive connection to the paradoxical ways in which the relationship is both fraying and trying to stay whole, not-me can easily threaten to derail treatment. It is crucial to remember that it does so in the noble service of survival, an overriding biological imperative, and that we must learn to respect and identify it, like Rumi's guest, and befriend it so we can take in its unexpected and difficult wisdom.

We must also be this pain's witness if we are to have any power and luck in healing it. We'll now turn to cases that illustrate the challenges and possibilities of working with multiplicity in general and not-me in particular. As we delve further, we'll see that working with multiplicity moves us beyond the consulting room and into the social justice world of combating oppression, marginalization, colonization, and polarization.

It's Not-Me, It's You!

The day before beginning a seven-year jail sentence for drug dealing, Montgomery Brogan, the white Irish American protagonist played by Ed Norton in the 2002 Spike Lee film *25th Hour*, catches his reflection in the bathroom mirror just as he notices a white-underlined "fuck you!" graffitied into its bottom corner. Like a dagger thrown back, his reflection begins a tirade cum soliloquy.

What ensues is an equal-opportunity skewering and stereo-typing of every subgroup in post-9/11 New York City. It is the quintessential "not-me" moment. Monty is enraged at the world. He rails at it and eviscerates it. He scapegoats everyone and the world itself for all the ills of his life, and marginalizes them all in one breathtaking swoop:

> Fuck this whole city and everyone in it. From the row houses of Astoria to the penthouses on Park Avenue. From the projects in the Bronx to the lofts in SoHo. From the tenements in Alphabet City to the brownstones in Park Slope to the split levels in Staten Island. Let an earthquake crumble it. Let the fires rage, let it burn to fucking ash, and then let the waters rise and submerge this whole rat-infested place. (Lee & Blanchard, 2002)

Left unchecked, the not-me fault lines of self create the outer earthquake Monty references, a scorched-earth diatribe that belittles, reduces, and oppresses. And like a leaking nuclear reactor, this not-me mutates and maims so many innocent oth-ers and the very world itself. It is the radioactive nuclear core of racism, xenophobia, misogyny, homophobia, and any other collective attempt at othering and marginalizing.

Surprisingly, after Monty moves further inward to his own core, moving away from a collective evisceration, he begins to call out his best friends, his father, and his girlfriend for the ways they all sold him out. Getting closer to the not-me in himself he is avoiding, at the dramatic conclusion of the scene, Monty stops himself from consummating his self-serving feast. "No. No, fuck you, Montgomery Brogan. You had it all and you threw it all away, you dumb fuck!"

In a hard-won moment of clarity and insight, Monty real-izes his own existential responsibility for his choices and the glib way he has avoided looking into his own heart of darkness. As the son of an emotionally underintegrated father who drank his problems away and was forced to keep his bar afloat by paying off mobsters, we feel the pathos of Monty's situation. We see how his attempt to transcend his material and emotional powerlessness by becoming a drug dealer simultaneously had him running from the not-me shadows of shame and humiliation that haunted him all his life. It was only a matter of time before they caught up to him.

When unexamined, not-me has the power to destroy not only ourselves but our relationships and the very world itself. As the polar opposite of psychological creativity and improvisation, it reduces, ossifies, and entraps any who fall into its grip, and it needs more of its own diabolical fuel to keep it going. As Brogan's character shows, it is also the root of all of our society's collective forms of othering, marginalization, oppression, and polarization, and we must be mindful of it as a cautionary tale to ourselves and our clients for the heavy price it pays.

Avoiding Not-Me at All Costs: The Shadow of Death

Not-me is the hardest thing—or absence of a thing—for our clients and us as therapists to approach. It is like the black hole of death itself; it threatens to rob us of our bearings and transform what could be creative and connecting—something symbolic or "thrown together"—into something that tears us apart. As trauma specialist Donald Kalsched (1996) notes, without conscious, related, and deliberate work, not-me threatens to become diabolical instead of symbolic and life affirming. What begins as a noble and essential survival strategy in the face of massive trauma becomes a weapon against the links to life and creativity itself.

Like Kalsched in *The Inner World of Trauma*, I've had clients who have suffered sexual trauma that have had vivid fantasies of slicing up their bodies section by section in order to stay clear of not-me. The urge to dismember replaces the psyche's natural balm for remembering, and the person feels exiled not only from the world but from the very essence of themselves. Psychologically stateless, they are easily taken over by the whims and currents of their emotions and have less and less power to engage in psychological improvisation.

The most heartbreaking way to avoid not-me is through death itself. Rob came to me on the rebound from hitting rock bottom. Now several months sober and religiously attending weekly Narcotics Anonymous meetings, before meeting with me he'd been using cocaine to self-medicate and as a last-ditch effort to express his long-buried pain and depression, but he had no clue how to put that into words. Like his family, Rob had become too good at avoiding his not-me at all costs.

A wrestler and boxer in high school and college, Rob was often typecast as a strong, outgoing, and ambitious alpha male, but he longed for others to accept and value the profound sensitivity and delicacy he also possessed in equal measure. Rob hurt deeply when he saw a friend mistreated or when he heard guy friends talk disparagingly about women. He loved taking long solitary walks in the woods contemplating the world like Thoreau and fancied himself a man of another era, a cross between Abraham Lincoln and Teddy Roosevelt, equally comfortable on the frontier or behind a good book.

Rob had always had a keen empathy, and if that wasn't enough, his parents had modeled and socialized him to be quite chivalrous and considerate to his two younger sisters. He was ever ready to modulate and temper his characteristically intense emotions in order to protect his sisters' developing agency and to promote a sense of equality between the sexes, as had been taught to him early. In many ways, it seemed as if Rob had all one would need to be integrated, and yet there was still something missing.

Despite all of this loving support and goodness, growing up, Rob never felt like he could honestly express his hurt, pain, and profound vulnerability and sensitivity. His parents had both come from working-class roots in Chicago, and their families had made ends meet just enough so that they didn't slip into poverty. Both parents had known friends and schoolmates who got caught up in lives of petty crime and squandered opportunities, and they prided themselves that they found their way out. Rob's dad was particularly proud that he had become a lawyer instead of the criminal he could have become, and his mother, a schoolteacher, unlike the many problem children she taught.

Models of self-reliance, perseverance, and hard work, Rob's parents prized their own strength and viewed their children as the rightful inheritors of this legacy. Unfortunately, and quite unconsciously, Rob's parents failed to realize that they had unintentionally cordoned off a section in the family psyche for hurt and vulnerability. Tragically, one morning they would learn of its steep price.

Rob's youngest sister, a promising journalist, had shocked everyone when she was found lying unconscious next to a collection of empty pill bottles discarded haphazardly by her bedside. Rob had just secured his first job as a Wall Street investment analyst and was devastated but, he told me in session one gray November morning, not completely surprised.

Shortly before his sister's suicide, Rob had been trying to share how widely his own moods could swing with his parents, and how he felt like he didn't know how to handle them. He felt as if he were subject to the currents of the ocean without ever learning how to swim, and that his emotions—especially the new and foreign feeling of depression—would drown him. Because he was becoming so successful and outwardly seemed so strong and confident, his parents didn't think much of it. Given their own shadow trauma of economic and emotional deprivation, they didn't recognize it as a real problem.

In another sense, however, there was a side of them that didn't want to know anything about it. Together, Rob's parents had been running away for years from their not-me, their unconscious lacunae of profound shame, humiliation, and terror. Without Rob's parents to hold a space for this, it became something unthinkable, unnameable, and unworkable. Internally, Rob recognized that he couldn't go there and instead, he tried to do the next best thing: self-medicate his depression through the regular use of cocaine.

When he came to me, Rob had no clue that he too was avoiding his not-me at all costs, and yet there was a part of him—what Christopher Bollas (2015) calls the unthought known—that felt it in his bones. Rob had always felt that, despite the many outward trappings of wealth, goodness, and strength in his family, there was something missing, something taboo that couldn't be talked about. He knew there was a place of creative possibility that would reconcile the internal splits he constantly experienced, allow him to have his full feeling, and provide him with a way out of his own personal hell.

It had all reached a crescendo with Rob's sister's death, which he hazily understood as a symbolic and literal way of killing off the sides of self that couldn't be tolerated. It was the fact that had scared him into first going to meetings and subsequently led to our work together.

Humanizing the Revolutionary: Not-Me's Hidden Needs

Alejandra was a social justice warrior and a force of nature. An accomplished Juilliard-trained violinist, a young mother of four, and a resilient street survivor, she was the child of immigrants from Colombia who had settled in East Los Angeles. Standing only 4 feet 10, I was always amazed at the speed, ferocity, and power she plucked from the heart of her violin and how articulately and forcefully she spoke on many a political rally stage for the cause of America's Dreamers, the countless undocumented Americans who so often hid in the shadows. With the quiet strength of a Mahatma Gandhi, Alejandra was born to be a revolutionary, an ardent champion of the voiceless, and a no-nonsense fighter for what the world had wrongfully deemed untouchables.

From an early age, Alejandra became accustomed to a background score of the percussive pop-pop-pop-screech of drive-by shootings, the scripted nonchalance of the corner drug deal, and the fear of a run-in with a gang member or, ironically enough, a police officer. For her and her family, nowhere was truly safe. She kept her head down, much like the petty criminals around her, for fear of being flagged as an outsider and an alien.

She spoke to me once in tears about the time her mother got into a car accident and she had to help her flee the scene like a gang member bleeding and hunched over. The police report that to many is just a pedestrian affair was terrorizing for her and her parents, so frightened were they that it could lead to their instant deportation.

Alejandra found sanctuary and refuge in the music of Bach, Beethoven, and Brahms, practicing diligently for hours as a way to express and carry the pain and possibility of her parents' long journey to America. There was something plaintive, aching, and beautiful in the way she could carry a phrase and pivot from triumph to tragedy all in the quick moves of a few bow strokes.

Alejandra learned to sublimate her greatest pains into her playing and her politics, and yet she wasn't alone. She had married a tender and loving musician who equally shared child-rearing responsibilities and supported her ambitions, hopes, and dreams. Although he was a natural-born citizen and his family had been here for generations, Paul was a woke and progressive millennial husband ever eager to share in carrying the cause together with his wife.

Despite regularly and effectively calling out the culture, its politicians, and its policies on its unfair treatment and marginalization of the many good and hard-working people like her parents, Alejandra was inwardly demoralized and discouraged. She forgot to eat, had little sleep raising infants and toddlers, and regularly marginalized her own needs. She felt there wasn't any time since the other battles were so important and worthy.

On the outside she was a dreamer and a progressive reformer, yet internally she maintained sadistic totalitarian control of her nurturing, feeling side. This not-me side was censored and inhibited so dramatically that if you were to look at her metaphorical book, you'd see mostly the black markings of nearly total redactions. As big as she was on the stage or at a rally, she was nowhere to be found, internally speaking.

One session, I looked at her and tried to speak to the innocent child she had forgotten on the route of her crusade. I could see her huge heart for the cause, but I couldn't see it for her own cause, and I had this image of a disembodied fighter. My right brain wandered to the image of Nelson Mandela, and I imagined what it must have been like for him to be imprisoned and how he kept alive hope that his cause was just and to hold on to compassion for his own neediness so he wouldn't come out bitter and jaded.

I remembered the poignant letters Mandela wrote to his wife and shared with Alejandra my desire to companion this imprisoned side to whom she wasn't giving time and attention. I told her I thought this side of her was in solitary confinement even though another very strong and powerful side had already broken out of the prison. I spoke gently and kindly, as if to a child, to conjure this side of hers that I felt likely didn't even have words yet for the deprivation and sadness she had endured.

Alejandra was at first dumbfounded. It had never occurred to her not to fight. After all, wasn't that the road that all revolutionaries take to peace and justice? Would she be a sellout and failure if she stopped even for a moment?

Our sessions became those little moments—hourly oases, she would call them—when she could for the first time experience what it was like not to fight the injustice and skip over her lost innocence, that other dreamer she never really talked about or from. We could dig a pipeline directly down to her child self's visceral needs for safety, security, and comfort, way at the bottom of Maslow's hierarchy of needs.

Monthly sessions were virtually the only break she gave herself in a schedule filled with practicing, breastfeeding, picking up and dropping off her older children for day care, prepping meals, and keeping up with an aggressive NYC concert schedule. But soon enough, as she was more and more sold on our work, she started attending biweekly sessions and finding that each meeting was healing her not-me and giving new life to the sides of herself that she herself had marginalized, exiled, and forgotten.

The irony wasn't lost on both of us that she had become the persecutor inside that she feared outside. Echoing Neruda's and Hoagland's poems, she was surprised and perturbed by how easily the psyche could contradict itself and yet also bemused at how far-reaching and wise it could be in expressing her many inner sides. Even better, Alejandra began to appreciate the gifts of this inside job of dismantling her own system of oppression. Thus armed, Alejandra felt even more fully encouraged to meet her own Mandela-self outside of her own metaphorical prison, a more enlightened, integrated, compassionate, and powerful collection of selves even better equipped for the courageous and creative work she had been dedicated to all her life.

Transforming Not-Me Enactments

When a not-me or bad-me issue is arising, our clients come to therapy to figure out how to make sense of and integrate it. The patient's symptoms and presenting problems often become the first signal that something is wrong, and it is our job to elucidate how this will be ameliorated through counseling itself. More specifically, we show patients how to befriend the various self-states and understand their reasons for previously dissociating from them and how to shift more flexibly among them. In this process, patients learn to develop greater receptivity and openness to their various facets internally and become more reflective on how to address them interpersonally.

How do we transform not-me enactments in therapy? We illuminate a focal theme—some main melody—and its attendant and dissonant conflicts by helping patients name, process, and experiment with the not-me part of themselves that was not allowed or sanctioned within their families, within ongoing social relationships or the culture, and within the therapeutic relationship itself. As a result, new modes of thinking, feeling, and relating become available for processing.

Ironically enough, it is most often the case that we as therapists have to befriend our own not-me and bad-me sides in order to help our clients do that too. Think of it again like the modeling we discussed in Chapter 2; we quickly pick up their signals and it brings us deeper into ourselves so we can better reach them. At its best and most sophisticated, therapy is an inside job.

This rightly makes us all uncomfortable, uneasy, and ever at the ready to say, it's not my problem. It's not me, it's you! If you feel that way sometimes, don't be too hard on yourself. It takes a lot of practice to trust this strange process of navigating your own uncharted territory. And it so often feels like you're going in the totally wrong direction to find your way back home. Therapeutic improvisation helps you get there, not just in one piece but even better, connecting to those multitudes again.

Don't Talk About Your Feelings—
I Might Remember Mine

Todd had just become a supervisor himself, and this week he was processing a session with me about his new supervisee, Beth. A second-career therapist, Beth was feeling overwhelmed with and chastened by not having the answers at the ready yet as a new clinician, and Todd could feel her anxiety swirling around her like an undertow threatening to drown her.

Todd knew she had so much more capacity and grit, and wanted to lend out his own as a gift. Having gone back to school later in his career as well, he keenly understood this nagging doubt, but he had also weathered this to come into his own as a formidably grounded and capable therapist.

Todd had considerable chops as a clinician, despite not yet having his full credentials. We sometimes joked that like a musician with natural talent and capacity, it didn't really matter that he didn't know how to read the music of psychological theory because in practice, he had it. But despite his success and status as a clinician, like Shakespeare's Othello, he still felt subtly beneath it all, like he wasn't the real thing. But this was only a vague and shadowy feeling, nothing that either of us might put into words at the time.

He came up with a beautiful strategy for supporting Beth's strength and resilience, having her conjure up the very solid mother she had always been to her children and bringing that side of her into the room when she was feeling vulnerable and scared. It was such an affirming and tender supervisory gift. But soon after the session, he came up to Beth and apologized, saying, "I think I've been telling you *not* to feel what you are feeling."

He intellectually grasped this at the time, but emotionally he was still confused as to why he had done this. It bothered him even more because it went squarely against his own ethos of therapy: allow people to be most fully themselves.

As we talked more in session about Todd's other feelings and free associations about being in the spot of having to help Beth out, he couldn't stop from flashing back to his own moments of panic starting out. He recalled one particular week when he felt like he just couldn't do anything right, and just as the tornado of inadequacy was touching down on him, on his last session before the weekend, he got a call from his new boss and supervisor. Assuming Todd had a great week with new clients, Todd could do nothing but feign being okay. He felt he had to "just hold it up."

At the time, he was the only one working in the office on the weekends, and as he recalled it specifically, the only black man in the building too. And then it hit both him and me together square in the face.

Todd had been pushing down the not-me side of himself that needed to keep it together, hold up his pride, and counter the negative stereotypes the white professional world might have of him as an African American man. Simultaneously, he felt the not-me of his own family's judgments of his vulnerability as both signs and proof of his weakness and defectiveness. Todd had always been an emotionally sensitive and perceptive young man, and he suffered many sleights and taunts, even from within his own community, because of it. A perverse form of double jeopardy, Todd unearthed the implicit bias and racism of the culture and the implicit shaming of his family of origin and community and how they all converged to condemn this side into not-me.

Todd learned to put this needy, vulnerable, and unsure side of himself away lest it be used as an entry point to abscond with his prize and his pride, his very clear gifts and inner abundance. He needed to protect it from the world and even his very own family because it could be stolen. I fantasized that Todd would one day share the beautiful metaphorical sweater that he learned to cover so well with his protective blazer of formality and gravitas. He was such a great clinician that sometimes I didn't even realize that I missed this self-satisfied boy underneath too.

We now could see clearly how the not-me in his supervisee had, through his own mirror neurons and right-brain connection, activated his own deeply buried not-me too. And we could say it now together, as if in a shared joke: "Don't talk about your feelings—I might remember mine."

Diversity From Inside Out and Outside In

Todd and I marveled together at how quickly the psyche could protect and prevent us from full access to the birthright of our pride, dignity, and compassion, and how glibly it could marginalize others in the process of maintaining our own safety and stability. And from this point, together we arrived at the searing truth that the embrace of outer diversity ironically stems from a comfort with inner diversity. And we saw just how difficult that could be to carry for all of us, how easily we all could fall short of maintaining it even as nobly as we try.

We must constantly track and identify the inner diversity as compassionately and competently as we do for honoring, affirming, and supporting diversity from the outside in. Mining this inner diversity like Todd facilitates a deeper exploration of how the outer diversity issues manifest and how they can be integrated more creatively and consciously with one's unique individual story.

Second, it is crucial for therapists to learn how to self-supervise and to playfully indict ourselves for the not-me issues that go under the radar and to bring them back into the conversation. They will be constantly stimulated and activated by our clients and will surprisingly lead us to behave, think, and feel in ways, like Todd, completely contrary to our own wishes and values. Todd would never want to shut anybody's feelings or voice down, but ironically enough, without an awareness of not-me, that quickly became inevitable.

It is most important to remember to be compassionate and understanding of the power and saving grace of not-me. We don't actively choose to suppress it, but interpersonal neurobiology takes over to have us join in with our clients. It is a sign of our greatest strength as empathic human beings that we are brought to this place. So instead of blaming or shaming yourself for having your not-me carry you away, give yourself a pat on the back for getting better and better at clarifying the places where you are most susceptible to it and the ways in which you are learning to catch the signs of it trying to move outside of conscious improvisation into mindless accompaniment.

Teaching Multiplicity

It is crucial to educate patients about the way multiple self-states operate and to normalize their presence. Patients do not ordinarily notice the reality of multiplicity, do not know how to work with it flexibly, and are understandably surprised by its disruptiveness. Like a car with an automatic transmission, the gears of various self-states typically change effortlessly and naturally without much fanfare, shifting nearly imperceptibly. But we and our clients so often forget that we are actually built like a standard transmission, and need to know how and when to shift the gears and what to do when things stall. It is only at the moments when metaphorically stuck on the side of the road—when bad-me or not-me is trying to engage the gears—that a patient solicits help in the form of a therapist's guidance to understand their own system of multiplicity.

We can see these stall-outs most clearly in the case of severe trauma. Remember the client I talked about earlier in this chapter who wanted to slice herself into pieces because of her horrific experience of sexual abuse? Conversations in session that seemed to be about gathering momentum about her work as a graphic designer, some new romantic relationship she was pursuing, or even a topic she herself had asked to discuss regarding her anxiety, depression, or trauma history, easily sputtered out into a breakdown on the side of the metaphorical road. The shifting gears of multiplicity wouldn't catch, and together, we'd get stuck. Just as soon as I thought we were free-flowing, with the rpm of her multiplicity humming, she'd wryly and curtly say she didn't want to talk about this subject or that what we were discussing was truly frivolous and a waste of time.

In order to connect the shifting gears of multiplicity, we'd have to construct fragments of her experience together, and take regular breaks, with me following her lead until she found a safe way to move outside of her threatening not-me experience, typically some reminder of flashback to the out-of-control, helpless, and vulnerable feeling she felt being subjected to chronic sexual abuse as a child. I quickly learned not to personalize her seemingly brusque shiftiness and instead saw it as her way of trying to regulate, as best as she could, her psyche's tendency to get lost and trapped in not-me. Stuck in a place that felt like death and hopelessness, she needed me to help her get out of it temporarily, until we built bridges between the self-states that had been torn apart by her trauma itself.

With trust and time, I noticed the moments during which

she could talk spontaneously and freely associate start to increase more and more. To my great surprise, she could talk about her artistic work and then pivot to something irritating about her parents and even talk about her difficulties eating or sleeping because of flashbacks. What before had been nearly impossible to string together emerged into a coherent and ongoing narrative. Instead of getting stalled and stuck or shooting back at me, space opened up for the links between her various self-states, and this allowed her multiplicity to be a friend rather than the enemy which constantly threatened to plunge her into the terror and despair of her not-me trauma.

When multiplicity comes back online, our clients are able to have a dynamic and creative interplay with the various sides of themselves, like that Bach fugue referenced earlier. They can be in the creative flow of their own experience and thus become adept at improvising within their own experience and in their relationships.

One client, the son of political exiles forced to flee their country without papers, joked with me that whenever his multiplicity came back online, he would hear that old Tom Petty song playing in his head reminding him that he didn't have to continue to live as a refugee. Multiplicity helps us become a citizen of the world and of ourselves again, allowing us, as Neruda said, to speak not just of ourselves but of geography; it enables us to come home again.

It is essential to remind clients that multiplicity is the rule rather than the exception. The unified self is a sort of illusion, a magic trick of the psyche. Like film itself, what appears to be movement is no more than just a rapid succession of still frames. And yet, there is such beauty, grandeur, and depth in what emerges from this art that it is no wonder we came to call it by its rightful name: animation. Similarly, the self-states that we are able to open up into and improvise upon become the still frames that create the dynamic movement that we know as creative and integrated living.

Extending the Reach of Multiplicity

While multiplicity is well suited to helping those with anxiety, depression, social anxiety, eating disorders, borderline personality disorder, and so many other challenges and disorders we see in our office, it is also equally applicable and helpful for those with major mental illness. For instance, in the movie *A Beautiful Mind* (Howard, 2001), there is a poignant scene when John Nash is slowly recognizing the perils and lack of reality of his paranoid delusions. When an innocent little girl appears, trying to help him stay behind with her, he tells her gently and tenderly that he can't continue to stay with her, though he is clearly appreciative of her attempts at taking care of him.

I've seen this work in real time, talking with patients with schizophrenia as if their delusions were just one side of them—with its own equal say on emotion and thought—and using it as a countermelody to their other sides, the more objectively real and neurotic sides that can help strengthen their ego. This provides two things that are essential and so therapeutic in their own right.

First, it helps the person with a psychotic process learn how to have an observing stance on themselves even if they are overly identified and emotionally invested in it, providing them with an almost meditative practice to help them have some distance and openness so they are not just swallowed up by their delusions or hallucinations. Second, it invites them back into the human club by recognizing how very difficult it is for all of us to reconcile the clashing, conflicting, and yet truly cherished sides of us always clamoring for attention and love.

Multiplicity's Gift: Clarifying Diagnosis and Treatment

I first got the call about Kevin from his brother. It never quite felt like Kevin was really with you, like he was looking over his shoulder for someone to get him, and it was freaking his brother out. Kevin was at the age ripe for a psychotic process, and his brother, a medical student, knew the cases firsthand from his rotation in the ER. Kevin wasn't making eye contact, and he seemed preoccupied in his thoughts, and when you sat with him, you felt like he was paranoid, but there was no clear signal of what could actually be wrong.

A college student who was doing well in his classes and generally well liked, it was an enigma what was happening to Kevin. As I talked with him, I too felt the presence of his most dominant self: a superficially likable and clearly smart individual, but one who seemed vague and shadowy. It took a couple of sessions before Kevin, who I too was almost sure was beginning to show early signs of schizophrenia, began to let me in.

He had disclosed his love for baseball and how much he had enjoyed being a pitcher as a teenager. There was something intoxicating about having so much control of the action in your hands, and being at the center of the field and of the team itself. Kevin also thrived on reading the coded signals of the catcher and sizing up which pitch to throw for each batter.

Kevin had learned to love baseball from his father, who had died young of an unexpected heart attack. It was the way he called his father back from the dead, and Kevin spoke fondly of his future desires to be a broadcaster to somehow continue his conversations with him.

While he talked about baseball, it was as if Kevin had slipped into another self-state, a younger, more relaxed, and spontaneous self dramatically different from the preoccupied and seemingly paranoid self which typically began our therapy hour. He would shift into it, and then just as soon he would slip back into that more guarded self who seemed to be looking over his shoulder and mine as if there was some sinister surveillance.

One day, Kevin surprised me by saying he wanted to share a secret with me. I was braced for the beginnings of some florid hallucination but was served a rather ordinary and ironically less distressing reality. Kevin disclosed that for a long time, in order to make money, he had become a drug dealer, and he finally wanted to talk about it. As long as, he pressed on, looking to both sides of the room almost instinctively, "you can't report me."

Pleased that Kevin had allowed me to connect with this new self-state that was lurking in the shadows, I was very deliberate about being graciously receptive toward it as the guest Rumi spoke of in his poem. Instead of asking or telling him what I imagined most adults would—that drug dealing was both illegal and problematic—I asked him what he loved most about being a drug dealer.

And in that moment, it was as if he finally had the opportunity to take off the mask of his paranoia and suspiciousness and smile directly at me. "I loved that I knew everyone and everybody knew and came through me. Besides," he told me, "I was really good at it too!"

I could feel his boyish pride. A seemingly different self-state, it strangely echoed the picture he had painted earlier of being a pitcher. Only I realized those baseball years had been a long, long time before his father had died.

Kevin's mother had severe bipolar disorder, and her father's death had overwhelmed her to the point of losing parental custody. Shortly after his father's death and his separation from his mother, Kevin had only known foster homes, and in that moment, I realized that drug dealing had become a way of play-ing baseball again for him and of finding a new family.

The surprising thing about multiplicity in this example is how it completely changed my emotional experience of Kevin and my diagnostic picture. All of the paranoia, preoccupation, indirection, and vagueness disappeared as soon as Kevin and I began to access these other self-states and made bridges to his larger narrative. I had never experienced such a dramatic shift, and it convinced me of the power of multiplicity in action.

Like a palimpsest, working with multiplicity enables you as a clinician to uncover layer upon layer of the narratives, includ-ing the narratives of the past that were seemingly washed out. It allows you to become more precise and contextual about how you diagnose the current and prior challenges your client is bringing and so often opens the way toward greater freedom and expansion in the therapeutic relationship itself.

To borrow our musical metaphor, being tuned in to mul-tiplicity ascertains that no melody gets lost in the mix of the work, but instead gets worked into the point and counterpoint of the larger score.

Multiplicity in Love

It's crucial to see multiplicity at play in couples, where the polyphony gets even more challenging and thorny. In order to understand the complex world of multiplicity in love, again, we will turn to clinical cases and movies to showcase the dramatic variety of scenarios we find in our clinical work: the good rela-tionship momentarily gone awry, the seemingly terrible relation-ship holding on despite the storms, the complicated relationship that activates our powerful urge to erase and dissociate, and the toxic relationship that seductively pulls us to mutually destroy one another.

Moving and Standing Still:
A Perfect Day Spoiled

The day Marina and Tuomo spent together had been a joy. It was Sunday and each had thrown off their work obligations, he as a physicist working tirelessly at the lab and she as a contemporary dancer staging multiple productions, to ride bikes by the Pacific Ocean along the beautiful hills of La Jolla. For this highly cerebral and artistic duo, cycling was the perfect joint passion: the paradox of finding balance and stability in constant motion, an evocation of the multiplicity we all need to motivate and stabilize ourselves.

"Stop, it's a one-way street!" Tuomo bellowed from behind, seeing Marina about to go blindly into an unexpectedly narrow passage he had mistaken once before, angering local shopkeepers and restaurateurs.

Looking back while going full speed down a steep turn, nearly teetering off her bike, Marina managed to catch herself and kept on riding blithely, but in her eyes you could see the chagrin and rage collecting. "Why does he always have to second-guess me and tell me what to do? Doesn't he know that interrupting the movements in a choreographed sequence can tear the whole scene apart?"

A Russian dancer who broke out of the strict ballet world onto the modern dance stage, surrounded by avant-garde music and technology-inspired choreography, Marina was exquisitely tuned in to the sounds, sights, and movements of her own psyche and the world around her. She described to me an almost electric capacity to notice the vibrational changes of bodies and objects moving in space, the precise distances and motions required to make even the everyday experiences of walking crowded city streets navigable or the quick movements in her tight kitchen in order to cut up vegetables, feed her dogs, and flip on the television without bowling over her husband.

Marina also disclosed to me some not-so-hidden anger and resentment at the many commandeering men in her family and culture who second-guessed women, particularly the brusque Russian taskmasters who seemed to exploit their young female talent. This smoldering fire, which often showed up in the Martha Graham–inspired flourishes of her dance, was fueled even further by a controlling and strict mother who so often denied Marina her natural sensitivity in the service of helping her find another more suitable and wealthier boyfriend following her divorce from Marina's father.

An intriguing combination of mellow nonchalance, quiet warmth, and exacting scientific precision, Tuomo was a Finnish experimenter continually searching for new rules and order to explain the universe. He often thought out loud as if sharing a data set he was polling you on, and while it soothed and calmed him, it completely incensed Marina. Tuomo himself came from a family of bitter divorce where the rules constantly changed and he found it grounding to come up with whatever provisional solution could hold the peace. Inwardly, just like Marina, he had no idea he was both finding and avoiding a solution to his not-me. Both were temporarily out of sync with their own multiplicities.

Tuomo would walk away from these dustups dumbfounded. Why couldn't Marina understand his attempts at helping and supporting her? Why did she have to see the universe in such static terms when everything—as he knew it—was constantly in motion?

On most ordinary days, they complemented each other beautifully, her with visceral sensitivity and efficient productivity, and him with his holistic gentleness and thoughtful kindnesses, but today their not-me erupted and each of their multiplicities went off the rails.

It took an emergency session with me to help them each put

into words the nuclear not-me threatening to destroy their beautiful day. I helped them each see that unbeknownst to themselves and each other, they were trying to play the scores of a complicated music, and each had become an uber-disruptor, messing up the pages and tearing up the score.

Tuomo's seeming protectiveness reignited the domination, control, and erasure that Marina's father, mother, and the many chauvinistic men in her life had perpetrated on her before she broke free as both a dancer and a woman. Marina's baffling disregard for rules that could make Tuomo's world feel safe and sound had reactivated the terrors of all of it—his family and the world itself—crashing down under the terrible impersonal forces of gravity. The irony was not lost on either of them that in trying to help each other they were hurting each other, and that in trying to ask for help from each other, they were both finding each other totally absent and missing in action. They were staring directly at not-me.

When we worked it through, they were each able to see how they could compassionately carry and support each other by remembering their good-me sides—their creativity, intelligence, conscientiousness, and resourcefulness—and by allowing more graciousness and tolerance of their bad-me sides—their reactivity, need for perfection and control, resentments, and fears. Most importantly, when they could see and express their not-me traumas in words that could allow each to save face, they could begin to experiment with a new story line. I could amplify to Tuomo the profound hurt and anger Marina felt at the hands of abusive manhandling and share with Marina Tuomo's poignant hope to fix what seemed a perpetually broken system that constantly made him feel like he was falling. As we did this together, we were able to laugh about what a lovely day they indeed had, and how next time they were going to ride side by side.

Holding on When Things Fall Apart

It's not easy to hold on to the constantly moving subtleties and nuances in self and others in romantic relationships, to stay with and carry the multiplicity that encompasses good-me, bad-me, and not-me. It's especially hard and noble to do so when things are falling apart.

Adam came to me in crisis. His marriage was holding on by a thread, and he was worried that it would soon break and snap in the face of their 3-year-old son, David. Married for nearly 7 years, Zoe was a marketing strategist for a family-owned baby food startup, an extrovert's extrovert who loved both the fun of sharing the goodness of the organization's offerings as well as the buzz of the lively conversations and meetings with other working women. Adam was a literature professor who gave up his tenured position for a combination of tutoring and writing so he could be a "full-contact father," ever ready to break up his day by going to the park with his young son and rotating it with writing and teaching in the early morning or late night.

In the early years of their relationship, they were a happy, playful pair, joking to family that they had everything from A to Z. However, the marriage started to unravel as the demands of raising a toddler intensified. One day, cleaning up around the house, Adam chanced upon a book on Zoe's nightstand, and the red-orange cover lit up like the oncoming flares of an accident up ahead on a darkened highway: *How Not to Hate Your Husband After Having Kids* (Dunn, 2017).

Grappling with the sting of what felt like an open-handed slap to the face, Adam decided then and there that if he couldn't avoid it, he could do soul searching and possibly decode Zoe's inscrutable inner world. Instead of hurling it in the trash or at Zoe herself, he decided to read it, and to hold on to himself. Even though he felt slighted by the book and what it represented, Adam was willing to entertain the complexities of Zoe's multiplicity.

Adam saw how tired Zoe was from many late nights being woken up by their tempestuous sleeper—she even joked with him at first that baby David thrashed around like Adam in the night with the many active dreams he played out on the stage of their bed—and how little time Zoe had for social recharging on the phone with her friends or even at the meetings she used to sarcastically complain of at her job. And he felt deeply for her struggles in taking on the new job description of being a mother, even one Mother's Day sending her a copy of Brandi Carlile's song "The Mother" (Carlile, Hanseroth, & Hanseroth, 2018) to echo the travails and challenges of being the one whose sleep and selfishness were robbed by this tiny, needful being.

Despite carrying his own challenges as a father, having been left by his own father as a toddler, watching the collateral damage of his father's affair play out in his mother's sorrow and struggle, and vowing to choose differently, Adam was able to see his wife's many selves too. He saw how she, like many other millennial moms, suffered under the avalanche of a unique modern perfectionism: the need to be a perfect, caring, and active mother, a successful, ambitious, and empowered working woman, and a loving, respected, and prized wife. He saw the strain and pull, and how unfair it all was, and he even found validation of it in the book that hurt him so.

Adam also knew Zoe's deep-rooted not-me fears of being a failure. As valedictorian of her high school class, the child of two happily married and successful doctors, and an idealistic believer in the power of her own charisma, Zoe could not tolerate the feeling of not succeeding in all spheres. As many resources as she had, her not-me shadow side of fear, powerlessness, and uncertainty was being painfully brought to the surface with the arrival of the unpredictable storms of David's toddlerhood. There was no better time to represent the juxtaposition of vulnerability and grandiosity that she had struggled her whole life to integrate.

Adam was willing to entertain and carry the multiple sides of his wife even though at times, in her exhaustion and frustration, she unfairly displaced her displeasure on him. She regularly pointed out that he did nothing to acknowledge her. He always had time to do the things he needed, but what about her? Why didn't he give her what she needed and make up for the taxing strains of being a new mother?

In short, she was unconsciously asking him to speak to, witness, and build up from scratch her not-me sides, to realize them in a way that wouldn't leave her so unnurtured and uncared for. Ironically, in her toddler's demanding needs for nurturance and spontaneity, she found the mirror for the not-me absences in herself that her parents themselves never truly fulfilled. Behind the seeming perfection of her family life was an unexpected crack that only came to light in the crucible of marriage and child-rearing itself.

One day it reached a crescendo when, in Zoe's fatigue, unhappiness, and confusion, she threatened to call the police on Adam for trying to leave the house with David before another fight erupted. It was Adam's worst nightmare to be pegged as the bad husband, echoing the not-me of his childhood watching the selfishness and callousness of his father's inability to reconcile with his mother.

Surprisingly, he was able to hold on. Instead of retaliating with jibes at the unfairness and indecency of her attacks, he used our work to remember that Zoe was operating from her not-me black hole and that she was unconsciously trying to pull him in. Unfortunately, as we've seen, our neurologically hard-wired empathy not only helps us to connect to the wonderful sides of each other, it also brings us to each other's deepest suffering. Zoe's not-me transported Adam back to his own black hole of not-me, feeling the shame, terror, and hurt of not being able to fix the broken marriage of his own parents, and made him feel helpless and out of control all over again.

To his credit, Adam was able to find a way to speak to the profound hurt, fear, and anger being reactivated by this emotional storm, and he was able to help Zoe put words to the understandable terror she was feeling about being a failure. Instead of attacking back and reenacting the terror of both of their not-me shadows, Adam used each new fight as an opportunity to dig in deeper to put form to his not-me and open a space for Zoe to see that she could be a wonderful mother and wife without being as perfect as she had been trained to be.

Adam took great pains to find ways of showing Zoe that the playfulness and spontaneity of their little boy was part of the healing balm for the side of her that couldn't trust in her own process and be more imperfectly real. Instead of her harping on the ways in which their toddler was out of control, Adam leaned in to how their little boy could heal her sense of needing to have it all together and give her tastes of the snacks of unconditional love she had scarcely known.

As for Adam, he found a newfound way of connecting to the little boy in himself that never had a father supporting him and left him alone to tend the hurt of his abandoned mother. He was able to use the experience to lend out more self-compassion for the sides of himself that felt powerless, frightened, and, like Zoe, wishing he could keep it all together. No matter the gravitational pulls threatening to pull them both apart, Adam held on to the central cord keeping their multiplicities in place. When multiplicity reigns, we witness the highest form of love.

The Powerful Urge to Erase

Without the conscious capacity to hold on to one's many selves in relationship, a powerful urge to erase the other—the relational form of dissociation and destruction—emerges. An introverted and autistic-spectrum client named Noah gravitated toward his passionate, impulsive, and at times shape-shifting wife, Lisa, like a moth to a flame. However, soon enough, their complementarity became the source of their undoing, and they descended into irreconcilable arguments and clashes.

She couldn't stand his incapacity to be more expressive of his emotions and his tendency to attempt fix-it strategies rather than heartfelt apologies, and he couldn't fathom the intensity of her emotional storms and the ways her past family traumas continued to haunt her. Why wasn't she more self-sufficient? Why wasn't he more feeling?

As in the 2004 film *Eternal Sunshine of the Spotless Mind* (Gondry, 2004), they both had profound wishes to have the technology to literally erase their memories of the relationship so they could just move on instead of weathering and negotiating the complexities of their multiplicities. Without the glue that holds multiplicity together, we easily descend into one-dimensional typecasting and self-fulfilling prophecies of mutual hate, division, and emotional destructiveness. We become drunk with the power of erasing the other in order to hold on to ourselves.

Both Noah and Lisa would find moments in our sessions when they reduced, caricatured, and erased each other. She became the volcanic landfill of toxic memories she couldn't let go of with Noah himself and her own family, and he resented the nuclear fallout that chronically disrupted the orderly routines he desperately needed to feel organized and stable. He became the egocentric and tone-deaf analytics guy who couldn't seem to fathom and have sympathy for her depth of feeling, especially when he was at the epicenter of her hurt.

It took skilled refereeing on my part to quickly locate the source of the not-me in each of them that was threatening to derail productively nuanced conversation. On his side of the equation, I sourced the ways the pyrotechnics of her emotions reminded him of his severely limited bipolar mother and how he defensively yet poignantly used his logic to find much-needed cover from feeling burned alive. On her side, I illuminated the retraumatizing ways his egocentrism echoed the neglectful emotional narcissism of her own parents, leaving her feeling totally invisible and worthless.

I could call back the moments between them in the here and now that became islands of conflict-free, good-me moments. We remembered together the many affectionate ways he reached out to grab her hand or playfully squeeze her, especially as a reminder of his love in times of great conflict. We called up the caring ways in which he stayed through the therapeutic process even though it could be so emotionally trying for both. On her side, we recounted the many ways she admired his intellect and charisma and how compassionately she could reframe and make adjustments for his autistic preoccupations and hobbies. As this opened up, we found ways to celebrate and reclaim points of profound connection, how they both enjoyed watching old movies together on their couch, laughing out loud at slapstick moments that spoke to each of their funny bones and how grateful they each were for how well they complemented each other. It wasn't easy, but the powerful urge to erase was more and more replaced by the creative desire to bridge. And what started as merely islands of connection soon became the mainland.

Multiplicity in Groups: The Microcosm of a Hundred Orchestras Playing at Once

Just as in our work with couples, we find multiplicity in full force in group therapy. Although a whole separate book could be written on group multiplicity alone, I offer some notes here on how to integrate our work above into the special realm of the group world, a microcosm of the therapeutic improvisation we've been illustrating at the individual and couples level.

Interestingly, we see multiplicity in groups on two levels,

both within the group itself as a whole, each member playing an aspect of the group personality—the diplomat, dissenting opinion, the spokesperson, the comic relief, the identified patient, and so on—and within each individual member bringing their own unique multiplicity to the mix. In other words, you can imagine the group itself as an embodiment of the range and diversity of multiplicity itself. And at the same time, you can imagine each person in the group bringing their own large committee of selves into the room, and attempting to have at it with the rest of the members. It's no wonder then that group process can be especially intimidating for the beginning or even veteran therapist.

At times, because of this unique feature, it's useful to analogize group process as both working with a unified orchestra with the same score, and simultaneously a collection of 10 or more individual orchestras, each with their own programs. It's like the old Jewish joke, "Ask two Jews, get three different opinions." It can be unruly and challenging, but when channeled and harnessed correctly, group process can be an enormously powerful, creative, and effective modality.

Groups develop in the ways we have discussed for individuals with their multiplicity, and group therapy too proceeds in a similar sequence, deepening from a focus on the strengths of good-me to the conflicts of bad-me and deep down further to the painful, unspeakable places of trauma known as not-me. In the beginning, group members gain a sense of hope, optimism, connection, and cohesiveness from sharing the good-me aspects of their membership status: the shared commitment to working deeply on a psychological issue like anxiety, depression, trauma, or recovery; the strengths that come with their special group identity, that is, a group of recovering substance abusers, of working moms trying to find better work-life balance, a men's group trying to improve their emotional intimacy skills, an LGBTQA group sharing their newfound pride in a long-awaited affirming and creative space, and so on; or the energizing buzz of the motivation and pride they feel in working together in the beginning stages of the group itself. This could be openness to self-disclosing, altruistically providing support to other members, modeling shared group strategies that showcase growth and improvement, or celebrating achievements inside and outside the group itself.

Over time, the group is taught to become more comfortable with sharing bad-me elements of their identities, the ways in which they or their disorders have led them to do or say hurtful, maladaptive things and how that might play out again in the group itself. Finally, as the group matures and is led by an experienced leader, they become more open to locating and giving form to not-me elements, those aspects of the individual or group process that go underground and need conscious work to articulate: the ways in which a young process group might avoid taking full responsibility for the content and flow of sessions, the way the group as a whole or in part can avoid looking at shadow sides of their functioning by noting how perfect the world is in the group as compared to that terrible world out there, or the ways in which group members can inadvertently silence and sideline wholesale issues of discussion.

From the start, Irvin Yalom (2005), a master group therapist and educator, warns against the two most important and likely not-me culprits in derailing and destroying a group process: scapegoating and monopolizing. Scapegoating is the active othering of group members, making them reexperience a sense of not-me and foreclosing the curiosity and compassion needed for any group member or the group as a whole to examine those facets of their multiplicity.

Monopolizing, conversely, is the overfocus on one person's story at the expense of the multiplicity of the group, draining the group of its necessary power to stay connected to the many orchestras within and between them. Both scapegoating and monopolizing conspire to limit and reduce multiplicity in individuals and the group as a whole, and as such they threaten to close off more nuanced, three-dimensional ways of understanding, exploring, and relating.

Happily, just as in the right-to-left-brain oscillations of our individual work—toggling back and forth between therapeutic presence and authority—so too do we help group along. Yalom again rightfully notes the centrality of process illumination, the process of allowing the group to fully experience in the moment the full measure of their feelings, thoughts, and behavior playing out on the group stage, and then to curiously and creatively reflect on what might have occurred and why and how it can help further group members' individual goals and the group's goals as a whole.

In an elegant distillation of the way our interpersonal neurobiology works, Yalom (2005) notes the importance of allowing the right-brain-led, emotionally rich, and here-and-now power of the moment to be the leader and maestro, and the left-brained discriminating, interpretive, and reflective retelling and representing to be the emissary and servant. Taken together, in groups, we have a recapitulation of the process we see on the internal individual level operating at our neuroscientific cores. And similarly, this is the central place from which the art of group psychotherapy emerges.

How Our Culture Loses Hold of Multiplicity and Descends Into Polarization

When multiplicity is not in play, we easily descend into polarization, marginalization, and division from ourselves and each other. Creative and three-dimensional relating is lost, and we lose the thread of the potential for something more to emerge between us. In short, we see the root of the societal ills that stem from a lack of curiosity, engagement, and openness to the diversity of our internal multiplicity itself.

Many of the polarizing issues in our culture right now are so combustible because they hit on profound areas of meaning and identity, dangerously close to individual and collective traumas: the not-me hiding in our multiplicity. There is no magical way to disentangle them, which is why it's so tricky and challenging to maintain reasonable discourse about them, and unfortunately, technology's instant-gratification platforms—Twitter, Facebook, and text messaging, to name just a few—make it easier and easier to eschew reflection and nuance for snap judgments and cancel-culture obliteration.

Polarizing issues hit our psychological buttons—the place we feel our voice isn't heard or even allowed at the table. When trauma is operating like this, a very valuable side isn't given air time. It feels hurt, neglected, devalued, or humiliated—so it has to fight to be heard. Unfortunately, without consciously working on this—either interpersonally or through therapy itself—creative space quickly descends into polarizing self-fulfilling prophecies.

We see polarization all around us in the political and personal spheres. As a country, we have a difficult time talking to each other about issues we hold dear. When we do try, it's like that couple who just digs their heels in further and further (Gottman & Silver, 1999). We all become perfectionists: I'm completely right, you're totally wrong, and if you don't agree with me, I'll find my friends online or in person to back me up or shame you for how idiotic your view is.

So many feel helpless and powerless to change it, but working with multiplicity heals these divisions and opens up a space for creative dialogue. Distilled down, there are four basic steps that will take a situation—in the culture as in our therapy sessions with clients—degenerating into polarization and transform it step by step from one- to three-dimensional relating again. We must constantly come back to these steps in order to make something creative out of the unruly multiplicity of which we all partake.

Step 1: Follow the hurt, not the hate, and hold on to yourself.

Polarization is a siren song that tries to pull us into the unconscious so that we lose a vital connection to ourselves and others. It sells us the fiction that one-dimensional perfection is better than three-dimensional relating, and lures us to retaliate with hatred instead of empathy. If it does take you down underwater, it will bring you up with fool's gold.

Step 2: We are part of both the problem and the solution.

You know that old rallying cry: "If you're not part of the solution, you're part of the problem." Be careful of this one—it's polarization masquerading as progress. Jettison this advice, and instead, start from the premise that we are all part of both the problem *and* the solution. To reach this second dimension of relating, both sides need to implicate and explain themselves. It's not just you, it's me too. And if you can agree, then we have the beginnings of something interesting going on. We begin to hold the torn pieces of a treasure map together.

Step 3: If we stay through this process together, surprising transformations will emerge.

You will both have discovered the true gold. Since you both made it happen together, you can share it and feel enlarged in the new abundance that is three-dimensional relating.

TRANSFORMING THE TROLL:
MOVING BEYOND INTERNET ECHO CHAMBERS

Where's a good model for how to carry our multiplicities and combat polarization? Surprisingly, an irreverent and bawdy comedienne like Sarah Silverman, an ardent and vocal champion of the power of psychotherapy for her own struggles with depression, fills these shoes extraordinarily well. Responding to what many of us would just call an internet troll, she completes all our steps (Klein, 2018).

After saying that she is open to hearing the views of what many considered a political opponent, a man calls her the c-word that many women consider the vilest insult in the world. Instead of retaliating, she holds on to herself and looks for the hurt, opening up a wellspring of empathy and compassion.

In a tweet exchange, she tells him that she sees what he's doing, that his anger and hate are "thinly veiled pain," and she wants him to choose love. Sharing her own parallel vulnerabilities, she connects to his pain through her own, creating an empathic bridge.

What emerges soon after is the man's profound hurt: He still reels from being a victim of sexual abuse as a child. He also has major back problems but no insurance to get help. He feels powerless, bitter, broken, and utterly disconnected.

Silverman helps him stay with and tap into his hurt more deeply and to begin the repair of his trauma—his profound mistrust—she joins in his defense against those who have violated him and lets him know that she believes in him, that he deserves to get even more compassion and strength in a support group and in therapy. She provides a way forward and holds out hope.

In the process, he apologizes for his initial insult and is amazed that she can see so much good in him. She too is surprised that she is tapping into all of this from just a simple insult.

In a storybook ending, Silverman reaches out to find medical care in his area, directs her followers to his GoFundMe page, and not only do people flock to his page, Silverman eventually pays for his medical expenses herself. This one word of hate became the springboard for a transformative experience for both.

NOT COOL: THE MUTUAL TRAUMA OF POLARIZATION

Accelerated by the merciless speed of our Twitter and Facebook posts and a culture fueled by instant gratification rather than considered and deliberate engagement, it's seductive to run to our own internet echo chambers to mete out justice when we feel wronged. Paradoxically, however, this creates more division and trauma, and in the following example led to rabid internet trolling, a flurry of death threats, and both parties getting fired from their jobs.

As chronicled in Jon Ronson's (2015) book *So You've Been Publicly Shamed*, Adria Richards, a Jewish African American tech developer, publicly called out two white men sitting behind her at a conference for a shared private joke that mixed sexual innuendo with computer jargon. She did so with a single tweet of their statement and photo, with a seemingly casual indictment: "Not cool."

From her perspective, it felt justifiable to feel so angry and hurt, as it occurred just as the speakers were talking of the challenges of being a woman in a male-dominated field and the continued need for reforms. With a history of observing men being abusive, violent, and demeaning in her early family life, her individual trauma was joined by the collective trauma (societal racism) of feeling marginalized in her field as a woman of color. Happening in real time again, it felt unbearable.

This perfect storm of emotionally loaded material was quickly and defensively organized into a narrative about the men's malicious intent to be misogynistic and destructive. Furthermore, she felt mobilized to protect not only herself but also other women and the future of programming itself. To her, this was social justice at its finest.

Rather than being able to talk about and process this hate and hurt, though, she sent out a tweet outing their behavior to the rest of the world so that they could be called to justice. Adria shamed and degraded the men without understanding where they themselves might be coming from, that is, not recognizing and making room for their subjectivity. Her response essentially gave her trauma over to them rather than truly working it through for herself and with them.

For their part, the men felt they were saying something innocuous, not having the traumatic background of feeling marginalized as a woman of color or a personal history of abuse. Nor did they realize that anybody would be measuring their words so carefully in what was intended to be a private conversation. Simply put, they didn't maliciously intend their inside joke to undermine the personal or communal safety of the space.

If they were guilty of being ignorant or insensitive, when held to account on it, they were apologetic about its unintended consequences later. Because they were not given an opportunity to speak, however, they quickly became enmeshed in a traumatic spiral. Sealing the deal on a retaliatory countertraumatization, one of the men was subsequently fired from his job.

If polarizing events like this are not noticed and worked through with reflection and empathic availability, they easily degenerate into mutual traumatization, where each person becomes a walking judge, jury, and executioner. The men in this example now got to feel the same kind of demeaning and dehumanizing treatment that they had reactivated, and also had no words or recourse of action that could help it. They were subjected to the powerlessness and ruthlessness of trauma itself.

WE DO IT TOGETHER:
THE PRIZE AFTER POLARIZATION

Check out the following unexpected and refreshing contrast (Soong, 2017). A Black Lives Matter leader attends a Trump rally—the mother of all rallies—and a surprise occurs. In front of his seeming enemies, organizer and Trump supporter Tommy Gunn invites the BLM leader, Hawk Newsome, to the stage.

Gunn says the rally is to end violence and celebrate America, where there is true freedom to express oneself and have the right to agree or disagree on both sides. In this simple but powerful move, he genuinely opens the door for listening rather than the knee-jerk reaction of hatred, allowing for expressions of hurt and, even better, a space for dialogue.

The BLM leader talks about being an American too, echoing de Tocqueville (Toqueville, Mansfield, & Winthrop, 2000) who said, "The greatness of America lies not in being more enlightened than any other nation, but rather in her ability to repair her faults." He shares the desire to fix something broken, the hurt he feels in seeing black people disproportionately killed, of little happening to stop it or mete out justice. When interrupted with objections of anger and hate—that cops matter too, that all lives matter—Newsome listens and addresses the hurt, becoming a compassionate witness for his detractors while holding on to himself and clarifying his position.

He is able to connect to the other side's concerns, but then he does something miraculous, saying, "If we really want America great, we do it together!" Highlighting the fact that we can only do this in creative collaboration, he appeals to the process that has been a distinctively American one: the political engagement of equals in dialogue.

In this lovely example, we see each side following the hurt

rather than the hate, of holding on and witnessing each other, recognizing that both are part of the problem and solution together. The sweetest surprise came at the end of Newsome's speech when he was asked by a fierce Trump supporter if he could get a picture of him alongside his blond-haired, blue-eyed little boy.

BUILDING THE CREATIVE BRIDGE

It is striking how close the healing and growing areas, internally speaking, are to places of great torment and pain. To stay in the creative territory is to bridge them through some new shared form, one that provides the most satisfying and long-lasting antidote to polarization's stubborn attempts, like trauma itself, to reframe both the present and future as the long-feared past. It is only through that courageous process that we become equals again, and that the possibility and pursuit of happiness becomes our reality together.

Conclusion

Tracking and translating multiplicity is at the heart of successful therapeutic improvisation. It is a full-contact sport that calls for our most profound intellectual and emotional creativity and resourcefulness. And yet our continued practice and facility with the many intricate scales of interpersonal neurobiology enables us to weave together many interesting melodies and harmonies both in ourselves and in our patients. Consequently, this often challenging work also becomes its own intriguing and unexpected reward. Like that mysteriously beautiful fugue, it feels like something is no longer running away from us but instead is just about to take flight and soar in our very hands.

EXERCISE 1: Working With Multiplicity

As we work with multiplicity with our patients, it is best to approach them as Shakespearean characters, with unexpected dimensions and layering that can make them even more interesting. Shakespeare has a knack for showing us the poignant sides of villains and the darker sides of heroes as well as showcasing how maddeningly complex it is to be human in the first place. Whether it is Othello's great success, status, and pride on the one hand, and his profound insecurity, feelings of marginalization, and shame on the other, we can see many dimensions. As his foil, we can also see Iago, the devious architect of Othello's downfall, as a sad, envious, and unhappy man looking for his own unactualized desires.

BREAKING IT DOWN TO BUILD IT BACK UP

It's easiest to break down multiplicity into its components: good-me, bad-me, and not-me. Good-me is all of the selves that we consider virtuous, positive, and pleasing, and note that they are usually seen that way first by parents, teachers, and society as well. Bad-me sides are the selves we or our caretakers view as unsavory, irritating, or embarrassing. Not-me sides are those we consider utterly mortifying, terrifying, humiliating, negating, and annihilating. They are the psychological kryptonite that threatens to completely disable us. And remember, just as for Superman, this kryptonite, when we look closely enough, is a piece of our very own planet or homeland, something from our past that is so grievously painful that we can hardly look it in the eye without becoming completely frozen and petrified. It is a cruel irony that what can so unmoor us is a hidden piece of home.

MIRROR, MIRROR ON THE WALL, WHO'S THE FAIREST OF THEM ALL?

Recognizing good-me qualities often fits easily into a strengths-based approach to therapy, easing into the difficult stuff by first getting to know what is solid. Good-me qualities run the gamut from resilient to resourceful, hardworking, attractive, intelligent, funny, adventurous, diplomatic, cheerful, deliberate, detail-oriented—an endless list of personal adjectives to describe what we love about ourselves and, even more importantly, what was loved, fostered, and sanctioned by our caretakers.

As in the case of Nick in Chapter 2, good-me can also be surprising and peculiarly connected to certain family, religious, or cultural values, what I term subjective versus objective good-me. For instance, Nick's pride in "killing with kindness" or the very religious person's pride in their martyr-like generosity. Even with good-me, it's important to know the full context and harmonic resonance of the good-me feature. That seemingly sunny cheerfulness can be a virtue in one way but can also lead to a denial or minimization of necessary sadness and despair in another way.

- What am I picking up as my patient's good-me sides?
- Are they objective good-me sides or subjective ones, or both?
- Do they have any history of support and encouragement, or are they connected to any positive identifications or counteridentifications?
- Do they have shadow sides that the client only hazily knows about?

Lindsay is enamored of her good-me conscientiousness, organizational prowess, and success. These are objectively positive and constructive qualities. They are adaptive, functional, and creative capacities. On a subjective and personal level, they partake of both positive and negative elements. On the positive side, these good-me elements make Lindsay feel a sense of self-efficacy, self-worth, and pride. On the negative end, these same subjective elements make Lindsay feel that without these good-me sides in complete and utter control, she is not okay and not even herself.

The shadow side of these subjective sides feed the perfectionism that Lindsay uses to manage the bad-me and not-me elements of feeling like a beginner at times, not knowing the future, and literal and figurative messiness. She has a history of encouragement and positive identifications with these qualities because of the hardworking, ambitious, and can-do attitude of her parents. She has a counteridentification with her brother, the odd man out in the family who rebelled against the family's high standards and decided to be a low-paid stay-at-home dad who eschewed what he perceived as his parents' materialistic and bourgeois selling out.

Work with Lindsay may center around celebrating the constructive and adaptive aspects of her subjective and objective good-me, providing more permission and curiosity around her bad-me sides, and using the relationship to bring not-me into a form that is safe enough to begin to approach.

BAD TO THE BONE

Bad-me sides are the mainstay of most therapies. These often constitute the lion's share of the anxiety, depression, social anxiety, and other largely neurotic diagnoses that we witness in therapy, from obsessive-compulsive disorder to panic disorder, generalized anxiety, adjustment disorders, and beyond. Bad-me parts of self also usually have a deeper story line as to how they were internalized and how they function for the individual.

- What makes these sides bad-me for the patient?
- What objectively or subjectively about them makes them bad?
- Are there any hidden strengths of these bad-me sides? For example, does an angry bad-me side also have a healthy fire that can be mobilized, or does the bad-me side of sadness have a hidden dimension that can add nuance to one's character?

Seth was raised to feel that disagreeing or objecting to things was impolite and inconsiderate. This quality was so pronounced in him that he wouldn't even honk his horn at a car veering into his lane for fear that it would be considered heavy-handed. Subjectively, he and his parents felt that this was the virtuous and moral way to be; however, objectively it regularly limited him from being healthily assertive at his job and in his relationships. Work with him centered around owning the constructive, objectively helpful sides of this bad-me and allowing greater permission and support for him to move some healthy fire and assertiveness into a good-me category as well.

IT'S DEFINITELY NOT-ME; MAYBE IT'S YOU, BUT IT'S NOT-ME

Not-me, the most challenging, disruptive, and yet most open for creative potential, is the last category. These sides are often a result of some kind of big-T or little-T accumulation of trauma, either individual or collective. And it is our job to be very curious about how these sides get played out with us in our own not-me sides. As I've said above, it's crucial to follow the hurt and not the hate, acknowledge how we are part of both the problem and the solution, and to patiently cultivate a process that allows new facets to emerge. It has the power to turn our most resistant, difficult, and unlikable client into a whole new character, as Shakespeare does for his villains.

We've gone through a variety of cases from Jeff to Alejandra, Todd, Adam and Zoe, and Noah and Lisa in order to show in depth how to transform the not-me black holes into new creative nebullas for our clients.

EXERCISE 2: Our Multiplicity Within

Do the prior exercise with the utmost curiosity and compassion you would give to a patient. Allow yourself to envision yourself as your own Shakespearean character as well, and explore and explicitly state the various sides of yourself.

- Who are the good-me and bad-me sides, and is it possible to ascertain the not-me from your own relationships, therapy experiences, and so on?
- What traits and characteristics do you most value about yourself in your personal and your professional life?
- What are the characteristics you begrudge, consider a nuisance, and hope and wish people don't see?
- Are there any not-me sides that come out in highly charged interpersonal enactments that are attempts at speaking your trauma?

Allison was very attentive, insightful, and selfless in her personal life, as in her work as a therapist. She greatly valued her sense of service, and it was very prized and fostered in her loving, supportive, and socially conscious family (good-me). At the same time, she had difficulty allowing herself momentary and natural lapses of concentration in session and being misperceived as not on her client's side. She also was uncomfortable with selfishness or aggression in her clients, as in herself (bad-me). Much of the time, since these sides were more safely in her bad-me zone, we could work on them by drawing attention and allowing more permission to have them speak more than the more dominant good-me sides. On some occasions, aspects of Allison's not-me—a never-acknowledged primal rage in her—attempted to find their way out by unconsciously eliciting the rage of her boyfriend or even of prior therapists. By giving the same level of curiosity and compassion as she ordinarily gave to her good-me and bad-me sides, we were able to give them form and convert these not-me sides into new creative potential.

As Pablo Neruda (2015) says, it's crucial to know the geography of ourselves so we can easily travel amid the complex geography of others. And as we'll see in Chapter 4, it's also the highest form of self-love and mindful compassion to be able to start from ourselves so we can deeply engage the fullness and range of others.

THERAPEUTIC PRESENCE: NOT-KNOWING AND STAYING TUNED IN

Because of the many different selves in our clients trying to talk with the many different selves in us, being present is much more complicated than we might think. Rather than being a constant we can always rely on, therapeutic presence is a much more fluid and shape-shifting creature. And as such, it requires us to get more and more comfortable with an improvisatory mode.

Therapeutic presence, as defined and developed by Geller and Greenberg (2012), demands that we get in the habit of listening and tracking our presence and the client's presence to determine if we are really in a space of relational overlap. It occurs in the place where we identify and connect their momentary self-state to a momentary self-state we know deeply in ourselves, and this occurs largely in our right brains first. In the process of jointly accessing this, we create a bridge for new possible conversations within and between us.

What We Think About When
We Think About Presence

If you love someone, the greatest gift you
can give them is your presence.

—Thich Nhat Hanh, Buddhist monk and peace activist

Therapeutic presence is as elemental and basic as following your breath, and yet, because of the multiplicity of ourselves and our patients, it is an ongoing practice that, as Jack Kornfield says of meditation, "takes a cup of understanding, a barrel of love, and an ocean of patience" (Kornfield & Khechog, 2001). But we so often feel that we need to control and force this presence.

Starting out, so many of us want to feel like we know what we're doing, that we're not really frauds and instead are the expert helpers we've always longed to be. No one could capture this better than psychiatrist and long-time Harvard professor Robert Coles (1989).

In his first year of residency in the summer of 1956, Coles desperately wants to be an authority, getting the constantly pacing patient known as "the hiker" to slow down enough to allow Coles to work his therapeutic magic or—better yet—talk in private. He craves for the nurses and supervisors on the psychiatric ward floor to know that he is, pun intended, a "step ahead" of even his most difficult patients.

Coles is instantly smitten with his quick-to-conceptualize and paternalistic supervisor, Dr. Binger, who from behind his bifocals urges Coles to read more of the analytic literature to formulate the case and glean the dynamics of "treating the patient." In contrast, he humors and tolerates the affable but discursive supervisor, Dr. Ludwig, a man with hearing issues that make Coles speak up and slow down.

It is because Dr. Ludwig makes Coles do what we all hate

doing when starting out: slowing down enough to be with our own insecurities, inadequacies, and complexes and see them for what they actually are: the metaphorical cracks that Leonard Cohen (1992) talks about that actually let the light in.

We need this because this is the starting point for so many of our patients too. They need us fully present in ourselves so that we can be fully present for them. And this so often needs to start with being present with what is difficult, not with what is easy.

Dr. Ludwig reminds Coles that our presence enables our patients' stories to naturally unfold and blossom, even in their complications, like mysterious flowers we didn't know were initially there: "The people who come to see us bring us their stories. They hope they tell them well enough so that we understand the truth of their lives. . . . Each patient will tell you a different story, and you're an all-day listener" (Coles, 1989).

Echoing Dr. Ludwig nearly 50 years later, relational analyst Donnel Stern (2009) reminds us of the power of stories and the witnessing presence that allows us to contain and express them (and our multiplicity) most fully: "Narratives are the architecture of experience, the ever changing structure that gives it form. Without narrative, affect would be chaotic and rudderless, as shapeless as a collapsed tent; and without affect, narrative would be dry and meaningless."

We want to provide therapeutic presence at all times, and yet it is inevitable that we will lose it. Presence requires therapeutic improvisation par excellence, a capacity to quickly identify our multiplicity and speak to the right self coming up at the right time and to pivot when there is an unexpected mismatch between ourselves and the client's selves.

Presence is also difficult because it requires us to tolerate not knowing, feeling unclear, and even being wrong. It is a process-driven quality that is highly fluid and complex, and it demands that we revisit our own unruly emotions and hearts of darkness.

In other words, it requires us to hold on when the undertow of their and our emotions seem to pull us too far, and yet have the generosity of spirit and faith to let them know that neither of us will truly go under. In that way, it partakes of Rollo May's (1994) definition of courage. Derived from the word *coeur*, it is the heart of all the other virtues of creative action in therapy.

Presence gets tested all the time because we are creatures who are also built for distraction, diversion, and denial. Like meditation, it is not easy to constantly dwell in the moment and be completely open to its unfolding. Presence therefore is not absolute or perfect but good enough, a secure enough base from which to have a personal and meaningful connection.

So many of us wish therapeutic presence to be like stage presence, anchored in confidence and poise, but it is actually about learning how to swim in the strange and unpredictable currents of feeling, the deep waters that therapy so often takes us so far out into and away from solid ground. It's no surprise we should all be leery of going into these waters; they are often treacherous and stormy, but they are not without their manifold treasures when we learn how to chart them.

Therapeutic presence is an implicit right-brain faculty that when coordinated and integrated serves the left-brain contribution of therapeutic authority. It is akin to the highly receptive and tuned-in ear of the working musician and is the natural complement to the musician's execution and performance exhibited in therapeutic authority.

In an analogy that presaged Schore's neuroscientific work on implicit right-brain processing and Greenberg and Geller's work on therapeutic presence over 100 years later, Freud underscores the therapist's need to be an impeccable listener. He tells us that the therapist "must turn his own unconscious like a receptive organ toward the transmitting unconscious of the patient. He must adjust himself to the patient as a telephone receiver is adjusted to the transmitting microphone" (Freud & Gay, 1995).

Since it is right-brain driven, therapeutic presence is picked up by patients much faster and is thus absolutely necessary for the trust, safety, and creativity that therapy promises. Carl Rogers was spot-on in underscoring it and its components—unconditional positive regard, congruence, and empathy—as the essential ingredient of meaningful psychotherapy.

In Rogers's later years, he began writing about presence as a possible fourth condition necessary for human growth. While he was not able to fully articulate this in writing because his understanding only began to emerge shortly before his death, he hinted at its overarching significance in a posthumous publication, saying,

> In my writing, I have stressed too much the three basic conditions (congruence, unconditional positive regard, and empathic understanding). Perhaps it is something around the edges of those conditions that is really the most important element of therapy—when my self is very clearly, obviously present. (Baldwin, 2000, p. 30)

Therapeutic presence is also a fail-safe mechanism that prevents us from missing out on the riches of the individual sitting before us—their true strength, adversity, and possibility—and on the greater emotional and spiritual rewards of profound connection. As Robert Coles's other mentor friend, the renowned poet and doctor William Carlos Williams, quipped, "Who's against shorthand? No one I know. Who wants to be shortchanged? No one I know."

And so, much like the discursive conversations about love in Raymond Carver's (2009) short story "What We Talk About When We Talk About Love," therapeutic presence is much more multifaceted, ambiguous, and mysterious than we wish it to be. It is many things in many ways with many selves, depending on how we connect it together in the fluid improvisations that become the therapeutic relationship itself.

Therapeutic Presence

If you've ever experienced moments of immersion in a conversation when you feel so connected that you experience something transcendent, what Martin Buber (1958) described as an "I-Thou" moment, then you have a taste of therapeutic presence. Therapeutic presence is a sublime communion that allows us to temporarily escape our individual isolation and become *a part* of the world again instead of merely feeling *apart*. Through the subterranean magic of witnessing, we are able to see ourselves and the world through the benevolent eyes of a loving other, and as a result, we pay it forward by becoming reenchanted with both.

Donnel Stern (2009) highlights this central fact—ironically enough, through a science fiction movie—in his retelling of the 1957 film *The Incredible Shrinking Man*. A B-movie version of *Robinson Crusoe* and highly reminiscent of the 2000 Tom Hanks film *Cast Away*, the film tells the story of a man who is mysteriously targeted by a drifting radioactive cloud at sea and subsequently lives out his days in his inexorable literal and figurative decline. We watch as his wife tries to maintain him in the security of a dollhouse, where he is later attacked by the now giant and menacing household cat. Thought to be killed, the man is left

> marooned in his own basement with no chance of rescue,
> horribly alone, living in a matchbox, climbing ordinary
> stairs, each one turned into a towering cliff, with equipment

fashioned from the materials he finds, feeding on cheese left
to catch mice, having to invent ways to cross chasms that are
nothing more than the mouths of empty cardboard boxes,
prey to a monstrous spider he fights with a needle he has
found in a discarded pincushion, and threatened by a flash
flood from a leaky boiler.

At the conclusion of the film, when nobody can see him at all,
the man poignantly recognizes the strange connection between
the "infinitesimal and the infinite" and accepts the trials of his
life amid their blessings. But before all of this, we learn that the
man has been finding himself while losing himself through his
recounting of the story through his journal: "I was telling the
world about my life and with the telling it became easier." The
man reminds us that it is only in witnessing ourselves and in
being witnessed by others that we truly feel and experience a life
worth living and, in so doing, transcend our bleakest moments
of alienation. As Stern (2009) sums it up:

> Prior to constructing his tale in the explicit terms of his
> diary, he has become an object in his own life, a figure
> suffering chaotic, incomprehensible events for no apparent
> reasons and with little feeling. The emergence of meaning
> from what has felt to him like senselessness, helplessness,
> and despair confers agency and therefore dignity. He is once
> again a subject. (p. 109)

Stern's contention is that whether we are witnessed by a real or
imagined other, we are granted an essential partner in thought
and feeling, one who becomes a lifesaver in times of trauma,
duress, and adversity, and a life giver in the moments we need
to martial our creative energies in the service of something bigger than ourselves.

This is what therapeutic presence does for our patients. It allows them to be witnessed and their stories to continuously unfold.

Where Therapeutic Presence Began: Evenly Hovering Attention

With the practice of evenly hovering attention, Freud launched psychotherapy as the science of being·therapeutically present. At the same time, he showcased the importance of therapy as an improvisational art.

In 1912, Freud (Freud & Gay, 1995) developed the concept of evenly hovering attention as a method to guide physicians starting out in the relatively new practice of psychoanalysis. This simple approach was initially developed for pragmatic reasons, resolving the myriad challenges that arise in the sophisticated juggling act that constitutes the therapist's main tasks: listening and interpreting. It enabled analysts to free themselves from the superhuman task of being consistently focused for many hours of the day—like driving without blinking—and strained to the point of burnout, allowing them to see multiple patients a day without the need for note taking. Moreover, it resolved the problem of keeping in mind and not mixing up the many details of the patient's story—names, dates, dreams, memories—but most importantly, it was designed to keep the therapist in the present flow of the patient's experiences.

Cognitively speaking, evenly suspended attention—the forerunner of therapeutic presence—allows the therapist to consider a wealth of possible interpretations without a confirmation and selection bias, expanding the potential receptivity and the cognitive and emotional presence the analyst brings to the relationship. Freud's dictum encouraged therapists to learn something new and surprising about the patient's internal life and create a disciplined format within which the therapist can actively be on guard against facile confirmations of what is already known.

As early as 1909, Freud repeatedly encouraged analysts to "suspend . . . judgement and give . . . impartial attention to everything there is to observe" (Freud & Gay, 1995, p. 23) as a complement to the patient's fundamental task of free association. In 1912, he formalized this in a method that consisted "simply in not directing one's notice to anything in particular and in maintaining the same 'evenly-suspended attention' (as I have called it) in the face of all that one hears." He went on:

> The rule for the doctor may be expressed: "He should withhold all conscious influences from his capacity to attend, and give himself over completely to his 'unconscious memory.'" Or to put it purely in terms of technique: "He should simply listen, and not bother about whether he is keeping anything in mind." (Freud & Gay, 1995, pp. 111–112)

Similar to meditation, this technique cultivates a nonjudgmental and receptive attitude to anything that is in the present field of awareness and attempts to just notice and be with it. Furthermore, it enables the therapist to engage affect more deeply and to be open to a variety of thoughts and feelings, even when these may be contradictory or ambiguous, as is often the case in those who are coming for treatment. Freud noted that therapists must learn how to cultivate this habit and in so doing "catch the *drift* of the patient's unconscious with *his own* unconscious" (Freud & Gay, 1995, p. 239), echoing the meditative process that Jon Kabat-Zinn (2019) refers to as "dropping in."

Therapeutic Presence Defined

Therapeutic presence is the yin of a therapeutic voice, the mysterious and pregnant space that acts largely in the background and yet carries to term that which is most fertile, alive, and creative about the therapeutic encounter. Described by Geller and Greenberg (2012) as one of the greatest therapeutic gifts a therapist can offer, it is the capacity to bring one's whole self to the relational encounter with a patient, to be "open and receptive to what is poignant in the moment and immersed in it," and "being with and for the client in the service of his or her healing process."

Zen-like and mindful, therapeutic presence requires both an emotional and a cognitive capacity. Like an actor who can access and inhabit the deepest emotional reaches of a character, therapeutic presence requires a profound empathic imagination. This includes the capacity to draw on one's own reservoir of emotional experiences and imagine one's ways outside of it at the same time to feel and know the unique "multidimensional internal world" of the other. Our capacity to access and translate our own and our patient's multiplicity is actualized through therapeutic presence.

Therapeutic presence is also a cognitive capacity that allows the therapist to "bracket or suspend presuppositions, biases, general biases about people and psychopathology, diagnostic labeling and theories, in order to take in the uniqueness of the client" (Geller & Greenberg, 2012).

And yet there's something paradoxical about therapeutic presence. Just as we know it is difficult to describe the presence of an absence, it is challenging to characterize the presence of a *presence*. Because, ironically enough, the most important aspect of presence is in its negative space: the capacity to not intrude, to not know too much, to hold on without holding too suffocatingly, and to momentarily revere being—and becoming—above doing.

Therapeutic presence has its action primarily in potential—it's no wonder that Winnicott (2016) termed it potential space!—and it is more often than not that we notice it when it is missing. Philip Bromberg (2006) describes it as the background music that our most enjoyable and "good" patients provide and the missing ingredient that leads us to unfairly critique our other patients as difficult. He reminds us that we need to help those so-called difficult patients build presence together from the ground up. We miss it sorely from our patients when they don't provide it, but it's because they have felt the same way all their lives too.

Presence in Today's Sessions

While it is always optimal to be therapeutically present in person, today's culture has enhanced our capacity to be present in other modes as well, and these have a few benefits and drawbacks worth noting. During the COVID-19 pandemic, we saw an explosion in the use of teletherapy with online services, which enabled many people who desperately needed to process the personal and collective stressors to continue or begin the therapy so essential for their well-being. Zoom sessions have the benefit of allowing both verbal and nonverbal cues, and yet they also have the paradoxical effect of being so in your face as to be highly taxing for therapist and client alike. In unexpected ways, they can sometimes interfere with the less self-conscious free-floating reverie and attending that makes therapy truly flow. At the same time, however, they are a godsend when it comes to allowing us to connect with clients in times of distress when we can't meet in person, to see their emotional reactions, and even have a greater entry into their and our own personal spaces.

Ironically enough, telephone sessions are also quite effective in terms of therapeutic presence. Like a patient on a couch with the analyst sitting behind, it enables both partners to relax and follow more of the right-brained tone and music of each other's voices and the interplay and improvisation of thought and feeling themselves. Despite lacking nonverbal cues, the telephone has a surprising capacity to open up new modes of improvising together because it taps straight into the right-brained music of the moment.

Whatever mode of presence you are engaging—in person, on Zoom, or by telephone—in order to best understand therapeutic presence, we have to engage it like Goldilocks: to notice when it is too much, too little, and just right.

Overdoing Presence: On Being a Receptacle

When I first started out, I thought of therapeutic presence as a total negation and contraction of the self in order to allow the needed space for the patient to heal and grow again. Flashing through my mind were all of the traumatic narratives that led them into my office, the haunting presences of the past that stole the space their developing child needed to find their voice and begin to play.

I was completely phobic of reperpetrating that crime and felt that like Carl Rogers—or Mother Theresa—my role was to make their world safe and sacred again by attending to every need. I rationalized it as the silent Big Bang, the passive contracting that paradoxically might allow new creation to emerge out of nothing, what the Kabbalistic mystics call tzimtzum.

And yet, I also found myself feeling strangely like a receptacle, a container of everything that started to just bleed and blend together, so that I couldn't do anything with it other than feel lost under its weight. Not only was I loaded down and resentful of this, I could tell that my patients felt like I was unable to make anything new out of it. They were accustomed to all of this "garbage" already too, but they wanted to find the gold.

Initially, though, even my patients welcomed it. They had never had somebody be so willing to let them put it all out there and not retaliate or judge them for all that was inside of them. And true enough, they did get to some of the gold, the moments of heartfelt tears and deep reservoirs of sadness, pride, and love. But after a while, they needed me too.

They needed me in the room to share the space with them because soon enough, they still felt unmoored by not having a real person on the other end. They needed a sense of my reality and presence in my own way in order to be able to feel like they could truly bounce things off and feel a real and deep communion with something larger than themselves.

But it wasn't so much that I wasn't with them internally. In fact, I was brimming with them and all of the resonant places it brought up in me too. I was so present it hurt. But without a bit of healthy and well-timed self-disclosure or a capacity to engage the sides of myself that inadvertently felt pushed around by all of their stuff, I didn't have the right balance of presence for them and myself.

And, ironically enough, that's what presence is. In contrast to what Rogers taught as a limitlessly unconditional well of positive regard, it's a unique combination of healthy portions of that along with the very real need for you to be there and take up space too. It partakes of holding on to and representing yourself, and as we'll see in Chapter 5, this is fully manifested through therapeutic authority.

As for our Goldilocks analogy, this was too much presence for them and too little for myself, but definitely not "just right." Ironically, there are times when we pull it back even further when we unconsciously avoid being present for them because we can't be present for ourselves.

Underdoing Presence: On Being Neutral and Inert

I was working with Jeremy, a supervisee who was brilliantly insightful, much like a philosopher gifted with a capacity to see multiple dimensions of his patient's world from such heights, but sometimes a little too high up there in the stratosphere in our supervision. When he got into a room with his patient this week, a 30-something man struggling with his relationship with his wife and complaining primarily of sexual concerns, Jeremy suddenly leaned heavily on his therapeutic neutrality. In the unfair conflicts of love and war, he was going to position himself as the neutral Switzerland.

He became neutral to the point where he became so analytical and detached that he felt uncomfortably perfectionistic about engaging the subject at hand: How was he to know how to make this man's sexual life any better? There were so many very personal reasons for this; how could he even begin to improve it?

Ironically enough, the patient's true difficulties weren't in the literal sexual sphere but rather in the ways in which he was construing or misconstruing intimacy, his feelings of distance at the seven-year itch milestone of his marriage, and his concerns about surrendering when he felt he should really be in control.

He was a successful lawyer who wasn't accustomed to losing a case and instead relied on obsessive attempts at cross-examining himself for his own silly shortcomings. How could a man who was married to a woman he loved be having problems in the bedroom?

Jeremy, an early career clinician only a few years out of graduate school, couldn't really engage these issues because he felt an inner mandate to be neutral, not to push too much of his own feelings or use his own experience to get closer to his patient's dilemma. He felt it would muddy the waters.

I playfully engaged him through an image of the inert gases on the periodic table, noting that they were among the most stable of the elements, but they didn't allow for any interesting reactivity. And then I reminded him of one of Carl Jung's (1933) little gems: "The meeting of two personalities is like the contact of two chemical substances: if there is any reaction, both are transformed" (pp. 56–57).

I also explored with him some of the perks of being neutral, the way it allowed a therapist to be a sort of omniscient narrator instead of a fellow character in the patient's narrative, how it kept us safe and cloistered from the messiness of feeling. I also inquired into his own appreciation of neutrality, and he confessed that it made him feel protected from his many unruly feelings.

Remember how much we've talked about the importance of modeling in therapy, how essential it is that we lead with the right brain first? Being more present and less classically neutral means that we can encourage and allow them to be so too. We are showing them, not telling them, that they can take a risk to get closer to themselves, others in their relationships, and new creative possibilities in the process.

As a supervisor, I modeled for Jeremy something he might say that was both self-disclosing and still neutral enough that it might open up a new dialogue and yet maintain healthy professional boundaries. "As guys, sometimes I think we put a lot of pressure on ourselves for performance in the bedroom and that we aren't as kind with ourselves on just being curious about how we are feeling about our partner in the moment. But then, instead of allowing ourselves to feel that conflict, we just want to fix it."

This opened something up for his client, who now was able to talk about how much he stubbornly wished that if he couldn't make it go away, his therapist could, and how angry and frustrated that was making him feel. Jeremy now could also understand the very real pressure he was feeling in the room that was adding to his own inner concerns about doing right as a new therapist. He wasn't just imagining that the stakes were so high; he intuitively knew that something involving such intimacy and closeness couldn't be otherwise, and it scared him too.

In supervision, Jeremy also began to feel more comfortable about his ambivalence about trusting his own body more generally, even specifically when it came to being physically intimate with his wife. Without needing to express any of the detailed content of this in supervision, he could allow himself to witness and be present with the multivalent feelings and thoughts it was bringing forth for him.

Raised in an Irish catholic family where emotions were meant to be taken care of in private and sexual feelings were not to be discussed at all, Jeremy was able to relate and identify more with the plight of his patient, who himself came from a traditional household where men were supposed to be in control and consistently provide. By being more present with the ambivalences and complications in himself, and even sharing them in a thoughtful and emotionally honest way, Jeremy was able to really contact his patient and become a partner in thought again.

Just-Right Presence: Responsive Cocreation

A versatile and thoughtful young actor, Ben complained of a depression he just couldn't shake, noting that it would seemingly come out of nowhere one day and disable his whole being. His energy, motivation, sense of pleasure, all would be wiped out, and he didn't know why.

I wondered aloud if there were subtle triggers that were

accumulating invisibly and then clobbering him all at once. I even began to put together some pieces from parts of his story—a quickness to minimize his desires and distastes, a need to feel "put together" at all times—and while they were seemingly persuasive, he couldn't help but feel both beholden to and irritated at my suggestions.

Although it made him feel too selfish to acknowledge them, I could feel them present around the edges of our conversation and encouraged him to disagree with me. He said he wished my theories held water for him but instead he just felt like I was getting it all wrong—no offense.

Taking his cue, I amplified what he was telling me, that people didn't truly understand how frustrating, difficult, and very real this depressive cloud was and that maybe it really was bigger than him and not just an easy-to-fix situational blip. As I leaned in to being present in that register, Ben seemed to feel more present in our conversation.

I even thanked him for disagreeing with me, telling him how important it was for me to really get to know and feel what it was like to be him right now. I also noted that it seemed connected to what he had said from the start: that he had a hard time really being real and authentic with people because he was so quick at the ready for them not to be able to handle it, to judge it, or to dodge it away. It had happened again, and this time I was the culprit.

But instead of feeling too much shame for it, I happily fell on my sword and saw it as an opportunity for us to be more deeply present together. I even felt grateful because now I could see and feel very clearly how easy it was for me to embody the self-interested and even selfish sides that Ben both wanted to grasp and was afraid of at the same time.

In other words, I needed to be fully present with his dilemma, being a colluding and complicit actor in its re-creation and then, like a magician, finding the sleight of hand to make my way like Houdini out of his chains.

As in a scene with Hugh Jackman or Christian Bale in the Christopher Nolan film *The Prestige* (Thomas, Ryder, & Nolan, 2006), we can't give in to the natural desire to panic at being trapped in chains underwater but rather must focus on the magic they are inviting us to summon to help us both get out safely. Of course, like them, we often feel that if we don't get out of the chains fast enough, we will either plummet to our deaths or drown in a water-filled cage.

But this was only the start with Ben. It was a big opening in the case. He wasn't done teaching me which chains he was tied up in and how we could both figure our way out of them together. He told me about two puzzling incidents.

This past week he had woken up two hours late to go to work. When he arrived, he was characteristically apologetic, but he was also numb, just going through the motions. He wasn't really there at all. Later that day, after returning from a Valentine's Day dinner with his girlfriend, he was relieved that she was going to visit with girlfriends on the computer for Galentine's Day so he could still be with her in the same room and also regroup in his own inner space. And that's when the depression pounced.

He didn't have any idea why. We began talking about it like a clog he didn't know was there and that somehow his psyche had learned to shut off the entire water system. In fact, when he asked friends, family, or even therapists, they often gave him simplistic advice like, "But the pipes seem to be working just fine today, no matter that the water pressure is a little low, they still work!" But he needed somebody more experienced and capable, willing to say, "There's something wrong here, but it's more subtle."

When he tried to stay present with what he had been suppressing, he associated to feelings he had never talked much about. He was around 5 or 6 when his parents had divorced and around 10 or 11 when he learned that his father was to have a daughter in his new, other family.

At the time, he remembered feeling like he should be mature and adult in the way he handled it, and he conjured up an image of himself and his father like one of those emotionally intelligent men of the movies who deal with heartbreak with utter decency and tact. He had associated in particular to Colin Firth and the 2010 movie *The King's Speech* (Canning, Sherman, Unwith, & Hooper, 2010).

One scene struck us both. Colin Firth, playing the future King George VI, suffers from a disabling stutter that prevents him from acting on the royal family's desire to capitalize on radio's great power. And yet his stutter magically disappears when he vehemently protests his speech teacher's disrespectfully and provocatively sitting on King Edward's chair. He finally gets his voice in full command and can rightfully protest.

It dawned on me that I was now taking on the role of the father in real life that he needed to both hold up and admire and yet also vehemently disagree with and rebel against. I had to learn how to become present with him, with this in myself, in him, and between us.

Nobody could be present for Ben's selfish sadness, his desire not to be supplanted by another baby, and his genuine and necessary hate for this unfortunate state of affairs. It made me think of one of my—and coincidentally his—favorite children's books, *Where the Wild Things Are* (Sendak, 1984). Like Max in the story, Ben needed to feel his wild side, the side that wanted to run amok in his wolf costume, stalking the family dog with a fork, crying, "I'll eat you up!" But it wasn't out of a sense of mischief—the bad-me and not-me elements he was suppressing—but a wish to eat the whole world up with his own healthy and voracious desire—the new, emerging integration coming online in our work.

In the story, Max has an experience of being met and companioned in his wildness and, even better, being anointed king of all wild things. For Ben, it was the opposite. His story was as if Max had come out of his room profusely apologizing for running after the dog and promising to be a good boy.

Max's capacity to disagree and rebel isn't met with full-throttle disapproval. It engages him in an internal journey, his bedroom transforming slowly into a forest and then an ocean where he sails in his personal boat to where the wild things are. Max has an experience of being present with his wildness rather than his badness and is even able to tame it by commanding, "Be still." He gently parts with the excesses of his selfish wildness by remembering others that he loves back home.

Not so for Ben. In order to stay connected, he needed to grow up and out of this selfish and wild side so his father and mother wouldn't feel like they were bad for subjecting him to the pain of it in the first place. Here was where those metaphorical chains first began to be tied around him.

Now, it made so much sense that Ben felt trapped when trying to find his space alongside his girlfriend and having to do his job even when he felt totally disconnected. Ben's intermittent bouts of depression had been the loudest silent protest imaginable, and placed so casually that it was almost impossible to find their source, like that tricky clog, the first metaphor that helped us along the trail.

Feeling again that he needed to be a good boy at work and a good man for his girlfriend, he swallowed down the profound sadness and existential despair that was hiding in his not-me self. He held it by himself until it could be made present between and within us.

Ben had avoided this for so long by capitalizing on his good-me side to manage it and keep him safe. He was so proud of the way that for much of his day, he was able to transcend this paralyzing depression and use his acting prowess to mask it. By delving deeper into his own personal performance, he could ironically be like Max, a secret king of all wild things. Unfortunately, Ben felt like he had the power to use his happy and energized self for others but that slowly it was draining his life away, leaving him gasping for air like the magician in chains trapped in the cage full of water.

It was vital now that we could be present for and carry his suffering. By being present in it and with it, we could lift it and bring together meaningful strands of his story that had heretofore never been connected, and this would bring him back.

Quoting from Peter Shaffer's play *Equus* (1973), when a nurse is begging a psychiatrist to overmedicate and subdue an anguished boy who's been institutionalized, the doctor responds decisively and wisely: "Look . . . to go through life and call it yours—your life—you first have to get your own pain. Pain that's unique to you. You can't just dip into the common bin and say 'That's enough!' "

We found and discovered Ben's pain together and, in our responsive cocreating, we wrote a new story line.

Our Presence Becomes Their Presence

The following scenarios teach us something essential about presence. Ironically, as Carl Rogers demonstrated, our presence with our patients starts with our presence with ourselves. The capacity to be congruent, authentic, and emotionally tuned in happens only when we are humbly and masterfully in touch with our own multiplicity.

And interestingly enough, the responsiveness that we bestow upon our patients stems first from the responsiveness that we lend ourselves. It is as Erich Fromm (1956) said of love: The capacity to love another deeply stems from the capacity for self-love. We might call this therapist responsiveness to the self, and it is the foundation of responsiveness for the patient.

Presence is a specialized form of empathy. As Hatcher (2015) notes, empathy is not just about being able to identify and locate the emotions and perspective of another; it is also the emotional capacity to regulate ourselves in order to stay connected. It is a capacity to tolerate the discomfort and modulate the arousal that so regularly occurs from taking on the intense feelings of our patients. And even more than this, it is being able to imagine and explore with our clients and supervisors the inadvertent role we may have played in the relational rupture or impasse in the first place.

Friedlander (2015) reminds us that we need to reassure supervisees that these ruptures, though they feel like mistakes and failures, are a normal and inevitable part of the process. In my view, they are the shifting demands of multiplicity, requiring us to keep up with being present for all of the sides of self that need to be heard and seen.

In short, therapist responsiveness is the verb form of therapeutic presence. It is the internal, active process of tracking the lightning-fast changes that occur in relational work that require us to become better and better at therapeutic improvisation.

When we give our own presence away too much and feel like a receptacle, as in our first example, we lose hold of bringing those sides of us to the table with the patient so they can have an embodied and real encounter that might even include some negotiation and compromise. In this way, we typecast ourselves into one overriding role of the totally benevolent, all-giving helper. This is a wonderful ideal or vanishing point for our work, but in practice, it keeps us too limited in the room, not able to model and draw on the variety of multiple selves within us. Even though this takes care of the patient impeccably in many ways, it ironically will leave them stranded and alone in others.

When we hold back ourselves, stay in our neutral and professional role, and do not tap internally into our other sides, especially our own struggle and vulnerability, we also prevent the patient from feeling our full presence. And this limits their capacity to find theirs, leading to an inert experience that often leads them to say they don't really know what else to talk about.

It is a paradox that the ideal situation is for us to be with the real, the fluid back and forth of a conversation that touches on this side and that, and inevitably comes to a rupture that becomes the opening for new creative work. Freud's initial concept of therapy was that it should be a form of free association wherein the patient could spontaneously and playfully share all going on inside, and the therapist would serve as a facilitator to traverse the blocks or inhibitions that inevitably came up. It was, in short, a specialized form of mutual improvisation.

Although we ourselves, in our own lack of full presence, can be that block, we are also the vehicle through which we bring the connection back. Again, Freud so wisely foresaw the ways in which interpersonal neurobiology operates, noting how the problem—the challenge of remaining consistently present—contains the very solution: the capacity to find it again. In discussing evenly hovering attention, our forerunner of therapeutic presence, he noted (Freud & Gay, 1995). "Just as the receiver converts back into sound waves the electric oscillations in the telephone line . . . so the doctor's unconscious is able, from the derivatives of the unconscious which are communicated to him, to reconstruct that unconscious which has determined the patient's free associations" (p. 360).

Therapist responsiveness—the active and embodied expression of our therapeutic presence—plays a more important role in therapeutic success than theoretical orientation or allegiance (Wampold, 2001) and it is the dynamic driver of the creative unfolding that is therapy itself. Learned through modeling and by being modeled, the dynamic duo of therapeutic presence and therapist responsiveness form the beating heart of therapy. Together, they set the stage for therapeutic authority, to which we turn next.

EXERCISE 1: Troubleshooting Your Therapeutic Presence

When you reflect on your caseload of clients, do you find yourself being over- or under-present with them? It's okay! We all need to go through this process in order to fully integrate our therapeutic presence.

AM I OVER-PRESENT?

A tipoff when you are over-present is that you are feeling unusually drained, tired, overly emotional, or resentful. You may even be feeling ignored, unimportant, irrelevant, or invisible, as if you could be replaced with another warm empathic body or an artificial intelligence robot, and things would still just carry on.

Here's what may be happening under the surface that will help you recalibrate your presence. As usual, it will involve working deeply with the client's and our multiplicities, the source of the quick right-brain changes so essential to our improvisations.

Is it a not-me or bad-me element in my patient or myself that I want to protect and keep as good-me?

Is it something in them? Even though it's a little uncomfortable, it is very important to notice if you are anxious, fearful, or conflicted about being too present based on what you are picking up in your client. Maybe it's a history of abuse, neglect, mistreatment, or some ambivalence around an issue you are unconsciously helping them avoid. If so, you can use your own feelings here as an entry point into discussing ways of providing safety, permission, and curiosity about an issue that feels rather important, charged, and tender.

Is it something in my role as therapist? It is also crucial to determine if your anxiety and conflict is based on your own desires and wishes not to be another hurtful object in their lives. Do I need to be the good object at all times and is this preventing me from digging in deeper to what needs to be worked on?

Is it something in me personally? It is especially valuable to be aware and do one's own therapy work around the possible ways in our own lives that we have been made to feel unimportant, irrelevant, or invisible in our families of origin, in our friendships, romantic and professional relationships, or in our cultural, racial, ethnic, or sexual orientation identities. Might we then be allowing ourselves to be marginalized yet again in session by holding back too much? It is crucial to hold the tension of how these might have been placed or imposed on us and how they become unconsciously internalized and replayed with clients. Above all, compassion, insight, and presence for all sides of this dilemma are the way back into our full multiplicity.

AM I UNDER-PRESENT?

A tipoff when you are under-present is that you feel like you are not really getting anywhere with the client, that the conversation is losing its emotional and personal charge, like there's nothing more to say and you feel like you're pulling teeth just to get more. Ironically, we often might see our under-presence in the counterreaction of the patient and mistakenly blame them first—they aren't really ready for treatment or this kind of treatment, we might say inside ourselves or even share with them. Usually, this is not the case. There is something missing and it is our job to find out why we are hanging back so far.

Does it feel like a not-me or bad-me element for my client or myself?

Something in them? Am I feeling and acting on their unconscious desire not to get too close to this material because it's painful, conflicted, confusing, or unknown?

Something in me? Am I feeling and acting on my unconscious anxiety around getting too close to the sides of myself that relate to and identify with this person's main issue? Or am I starting to unconsciously notice that the seeming peripheral issues—sex rather than intimacy, anxiety rather than relationships—are hitting too close to home for me and I want to unconsciously exit the stage?

For both your client and yourself, be patient, curious, and compassionate with allowing yourself to explore these issues without judgment. Cultivate an ongoing faith that by engaging the seemingly unseemly and negative aspects of themselves and yourself that you will be pleasantly surprised at new creative therapeutic work. Allow yourself to be an imperfect person and therapist, as it will engage you in the messier yet more interesting and creatively rich process-driven approach to being more present with more of their and your sides.

EXERCISE 2: A New Slant on Therapist Responsiveness

If *presence* is the being of the therapeutic relationship, *responsiveness* is the becoming that helps us deal with its complex waves and seeming tsunamis. More and more, we become experts at becoming more and more responsive to the subtle, complex, and ever-shifting needs of our clients, but sometimes we can forget the equally important capacity to be responsive to our own shifting currents.

The more we embrace our own multiplicity—our good-me, bad-me, and not-me sides—the more responsive we can be to these sides in ourselves with evenly hovering attention too. And this isn't just good for us, it's superb for our clients too!

Trevor Ahrendt developed a series of questions and an exercise to help us lean in to the raw feelings of our countertransference and formulate a better and more helpful plan for our clients. Being honest and open with ourselves about them frees us to genuinely like, be intrigued, and become more compassionate and connected with them, even in the supposedly tough or hard edges of their personality. When we are more comfortable in our own fullness, we can more easily be with and court their fullness too.

- If you didn't have to be such a good therapist and decent person, what are your honest feelings toward your clients? How might a more candid nontherapist friend talk about them?
- How would you feel if you were in a friendship, romantic relationship, or business venture with this client?
- Is this client bringing up a familiar feeling, pattern, or area of growth you're working on right now? What are the bad-me or not-me elements that it might be conjuring up?
- How might this client be good for you in working through this and having a new creative opportunity with it?

Ahrendt notes the helpfulness of checking in and having more honest conversations with our friend-colleagues, or "frolleauges" to allow ourselves even more freedom to explore these questions. If you are concerned that this is getting too personal, you can check yourself with these questions:

- Are the reactions I'm having common among others in the patient's life?
- If so, how is the patient inviting me to treat them?
- Are there reasons to be concerned that my reactions are very personal and idiosyncratic?
- If so, let me look into them as a space for more growth for myself through my own processing or my own supervision or therapy so I can better help my patient.

CLARIFYING MYSELF CLARIFIES MY CLIENT

Ahrendt also generated the fill-in-the-blanks blurb below to most succinctly get at these issues. If there is no personal blockage, you can fill it out with clarity and validity. If there is a personal blockage, you can use the statements to investigate what areas in your key relationships and trauma history are, like your patient, testing out something new and transformative.

> I feel _____, _____, and _____ about this patient. This leads me to want to treat them like _____,
> _____, and _____.
>
> This mirrors _____ and _____ key relationships in their life and reflects traumas _____ and _____.
>
> Based on those relationships, patients came to believe _____ about themselves, which leads them to behave in _____ way. This replicates the cycle, but they are using therapy with me to test that they can _____.

THERAPEUTIC AUTHORITY: OWNING YOUR CONFIDENCE AND MAKING MUSIC

We think of therapeutic authority as a relatively stable and fixed thing, but in actual practice, like therapeutic presence, it is quite a dynamic and improvisatory creature. In order to integrate it fully into our repertoire—to form a coherent and unique therapeutic voice—we need to be very attentive to the many ways in which therapeutic authority can be lost and found again. As in Chapter 4, we'll use a Goldilocks approach, sketching out when it is too much, too little, and just right. And as we go, we'll be most curious about how flexible, dynamic, and artful the process of holding, expressing, and exercising therapeutic authority truly is.

Overzealous Authority

In the beginning, it's easy to overdo our therapeutic authority. We all need to tap into our expertise and authoritative voice in order to do this work effectively. However, sometimes we get overzealous about it, subtly pressuring and cajoling our patients into implementing the techniques that will not just make them feel better but make us feel better too.

Rachel wanted her clients to be quick to jump in with excitement at the techniques she was learning, whether it was a dialectical behavior therapy skill that promised mindful reflection or an accelerated experiential dynamic psychotherapy technique that yielded greater emotional clarity. But she often found clients overtly and covertly rebelling against her assignments. She started to feel like they just weren't ready for therapy and, not so secretly, she felt annoyed at this mutiny.

As we explored it further, Rachel acknowledged that she never quite felt comfortable with being in limbo and in the middle of an unfolding process; she wanted concrete and immediate results. Her clients made her feel out of her element, and she hated it. She hated feeling like her contributions weren't appreciated and as if she didn't know what she was doing.

Internally, it brought out the criticism and perfectionism of her highly organized, conscientious, yet overbearing mother. She didn't want to be like that herself and had ironically hoped that becoming a therapist would protect her from this fate. Ironically, she was replaying the very same dynamic because her sense of authority came in a one-size-fits-all model: make sure you get results and get them fast!

It's a difficult place to "not know yet" what is truly going to be the most helpful for our clients, and so many of us wish, instead, that there were sure-fire strategies to help them immediately. Whether we are over-relying on evidence-based techniques, our theoretical orientation, or the particular sequence of healing, we easily forget that therapist responsiveness is context dependent. It is based in the very specific and personalized attention to our patient's unique qualities and our relationship together. It takes time, patience, and listening really closely to glean what is the right move in our therapeutic work with this client at this moment, and that is where therapeutic authority guides us.

Ironically enough, many beginning and early-career clinicians overdo their therapeutic authority, like a tennis player running around their backhand and muscling through with their forehand, to avoid the more amorphous and elusive therapeutic presence. Or, if it is our more natural inclination personality-wise or theory-wise, we will avoid presence because we rationalize it as less important to the overall therapy itself.

A good tell is when you are getting upset at your patient for not doing a particular therapy assignment or homework, engaging your particular interpretation more wholeheartedly, or even following through on the place or direction you feel the conversation needs to go. Why isn't this client talking about the underlying problems with their trauma history that are fueling their anxiety, depression, and general discontent? Why are they avoiding the grounding techniques that I've assigned to help them with their panic disorder? Why are they avoiding the positive affirmations that we've developed to combat their depression?

Overcompensated therapeutic authority comes from a place of impatience and fear rather than from one of curiosity and creativity. It is too concerned with knowing with utter certainty and shoring up our own fragile ego. Ironically enough, therapeutic authority flows best from the psychological sweet spot of high confidence and profound humility.

Not-Enough Authority

Not-enough therapeutic authority occurs when you can't trust your own instinct to choose which direction to take, which intervention to use, how to bring things together, and if you even have the right to interrupt the client's statements in the first place. Jenny would find herself intrigued by her client's multi-layered and digressive stories, her epic dreams, and her manic pace of selling herself on what she knew she needed to do to get better, but Jenny couldn't get a word in edgewise. She felt like she didn't need to, that her role was to be as epically present as her client was expressive.

In contrast to Rachel, Jenny had grown up in a large family where she was accustomed to people talking over each other and running roughshod over the important tender moments with a sense of rabid competition. It was only a matter of moments before someone else was going to take center stage, so you'd better go for it quickly, even if it meant metaphorically pulling away somebody's microphone.

We also finally made a connection together about something that was staring us both in the face but was not clear until that moment. Doing a number of teletherapy sessions, Jenny was working from a home office that looked professional, with the exception of one big thing: a life-size teddy bear in a rocking chair within full view of the patient. There was a part of me that always found it sweet and endearing in its own way, a reflection on Jenny's big heart, but there was something else that always nagged at me that I couldn't quite put into words. And now I had it!

Jenny felt a need to make sure that everybody knew she was going to protect their tenderness and childlike innocence. The bear was a stark reminder of that, and yet it also took away the perception of her professional authority. Under the surface, it belied a defensive aspect to Jenny's wholehearted identification as the kindest and most available teddy bear to her clients.

In order to help her sensitively with this important symbol, I helped Jenny see how valuable this bear was to her and her patients and how it echoed her profound and unconditional therapeutic presence. At the same time, I playfully imagined another side of the bear, a mama bear that could also protect her childlike tenderness that we could incorporate inside her and use as a springboard so she could more fully claim her own power and authority.

Jenny was amazed at how much this seemingly innocuous issue—therapeutic authority—enabled her to grow both personally and professionally. She was also happily surprised at how we could use it both to heal her unspoken wounds and also as a launching pad for new and exciting growth.

In contrast and yet in parallel to Rachel, Jenny counteridentified with being too disruptive of another's presence and process, and it pained her greatly to be potentially reperpetrating old wounds. In our supervision together, we witnessed and had compassion for this important side of herself and also helped her differentiate the kind of authority that didn't step on others' toes and enabled everybody to have a more equal say. In this way, we used the opportunity of taking on her therapeutic authority as a way to heal and creatively reimagine her professional and personal authority.

What Would God Think?

Todd was a talented supervisee with a keen ear for the rhythm of a session and the gravitas and presence of a young James Earl Jones. In this week's supervision, he asked to show me a video of himself and a gay black man he had been counseling with his partner for a number of months.

Jeff had been doing a considerable amount of work inside and outside of sessions, catching himself before he took unnecessary swipes at his partner, more effectively communicating the hurt and vulnerability underneath his episodic bouts of jealousy, and internally mending his frayed relationship with his father, who had been deceased for several years.

In an individual check-in session, Todd noticed that Jeff was having trouble absorbing all that he was accomplishing in sessions, and was beginning to feel overtaken by the bigness of it all. He could sense Jeff teetering into an old narrative of fear, stress, and worry, and, as if to catch him, Todd used his therapeutic authority to engage a miraculous sequence of self-rediscovery.

In a playfully nonchalant way, Todd leaned in as if to share a secret. "You're a believer in God, right? What do you think God is trying to tell you with all of this happening now?"

"Boy, you're going deep with that one," Jeff replied. But he allowed it to steep over him, and in a few moments of silence, a smile came over him as he noticed, as if for the first time, how grateful he had been that the course of his relationship had changed from constant bickering and jealousy to moments of genuine affection. He hadn't expected it to shift, and felt certain that he would leave Scott, but then, in a sheepish moment of confession, he acknowledged that he was lucky that Scott didn't leave him first.

Todd smiled knowingly, aware that the question had begun to take medicinal effect, and that it would yield even more as a chaser to the anxiety stalking Jeff. With a broad nod, like an authoritative conductor, he urged on the music he knew would quickly follow.

Jeff noted how difficult he could be, with his expectations for continual reassurance and prizing, and he was realizing that Scott's needs were different but just as important as his. He was learning a lot about who he thought he and his partner were and delving into them with much less defensiveness than in the past, when he might have made a sarcastic joke out of it all.

As if still answering the original question about God's

thoughts, Jeff marveled at the security and intimacy he felt falling asleep next to Scott, and laughing at his enjoyment of the reassuring sound of Scott's snoring.

"Even when he's snoring, I can't get annoyed now. It's being with him, really being with him, that I think God really intended. If you told me this months ago, I wouldn't have believed it was possible, but now I know. A long time coming, but it's on its way somehow."

Todd could sense the subtle notes of bittersweetness and doubt in Jeff's voice, and again, as if to meet it authoritatively and head on, he offered, "A long time coming is right. It's been so difficult to make peace with the important men in your life and to really have them and yourself together in one place. That's some big feat you've pulled off together with Scott, wouldn't you say?"

"Yes, we've done it here too." Jeff nodded as if to the floor, his eyes beginning to water.

"We certainly have my friend, we certainly have. . . . " Todd trailed off, allowing them both to steep in this moment together and take in its full measure.

Todd and Jeff knew what had been communicated but not fully spoken. As a gay man, Jeff had always longed for the love, approval, and respect of his straight father but never had the chance to work it through while he was alive. Jeff's therapy with Todd, a deeply empathic and secure straight man, allowed him to work through this very painful chapter.

The comfort with which Jeff now talked with his straight therapist about the physical and emotional intimacies of his gay married life was a testament to their work and bond together, and they both knew it signaled a very special and deep connection between them. For his part, too, Todd, the therapist we first visited in Chapter 3, was also profoundly grateful for the ways in which he could explore the tenderness and richness of his own masculine identity through their work together. As is typically the case, when therapeutic authority is employed well, it enlarges the authority and strength of both therapist and client.

In the sequence above, Todd masterfully used his therapeutic authority. He zeroed in on a question that could counter the magnitude of Jeff's anxiety and elaborate the scope and variety of his progress. His approach was organic, tactful, and well timed, and like a judo move, he lent his strength to Jeff so he could flip his anxiety and doubt into creative growth and consolidation.

The question, like a set of Russian dolls, became a question within a question, enabling different registers of feeling and thought to emerge: gratitude, relief, guilt, self-awareness, empathy, affection, grief, and reconciliation. Compressed into that single question was an opportunity to explore the there-and-then of Jeff's relationship to his departed father and the here-and-now of his relationships to Scott and Todd as well.

As Paul Wachtel (1993) teaches, our questions are often more than just neutral and passive information gatherers; they also have an authoritative point and a meta-message they carry along with them. And as Todd used them, questions can become both creative statements and invitations. In this case, Todd's question was a way of showing Jeff that he believed there was so much more goodness, beauty, and richness to Jeff's current situation. He was lending Jeff needed optimism and courage in a wobbly moment of self-doubt and sending the meta-message "I can see something bigger and I know you can too!"

It's ironic that a question—what we think of as our need from our client—can be used authoritatively. It permissively and compassionately opens up a space for a new layer of interpretation, as Itay Talgam (2009) tells us of the great conductors. It also demarcates where and how that space can be opened up more fully by helping the patient to zero in more effectively, but it also gives them choice and freedom with how to creatively approach that for themselves as well. In other words, therapeutic authority is not authoritarian, commanding, or dogmatic. It is explicit and confident enough to guide but flexible and supple enough to be open to a new creative moment together.

As you'll notice, therapeutic authority is even more effective when it is combined with therapeutic presence. Todd's capacity to stay warm, grounded, and available, both externally and internally, easily provided the space for Jeff to most fully inhabit and express the many shades of his therapeutic experiences. In short, it opened up deeper and deeper registers of Jeff's voice so that he could most fully encompass his multiplicity.

Finding Her Voice Again

Elizabeth came into my office with the winsome smile and bright blue eyes that sparkled on stage and then, remembering the comfort of the space, allowed the worry on her brow to settle in. She had lost it again. It was the third time this week that she went to sing a passage from an aria she was practicing and nothing came forth. The strength, vibrancy, and passion that she could harness in her soprano voice was missing and nowhere to be found.

Elizabeth spoke of how much she had been listening to her teacher's instructions, watching her vowels, gathering air from her diaphragm, and seeing the musical line float before her eyes as she began to execute each phrase. But it wasn't working.

Riddled with tension in her throat, her anxiety kept gathering to the point of a panic attack, and she was so embarrassed she'd run from the practice room. "What is happening to me?" she implored. "Can you give me any relaxation or breathing techniques or some kind of first aid for these panic attacks? I just don't know what to do!"

Elizabeth was losing her own authority, a perfect opportunity for me to lean into mine to help get hers back. But first, I drew on my therapeutic presence to really listen deeply. Elizabeth was definitely worried and preoccupied with pleasing her teachers, and even more, I could tell she sensed their own narcissistic need for her to be successful. Her teacher couldn't stomach feeling like a failure and unconsciously bristled at the raw and honest vulnerability that Elizabeth exhibited, and defensively told her, "Stop giving yourself away so much." It was a telling and prescient if self-serving interpretation, her teacher not realizing how much Elizabeth was actually feeding and maintaining her subterranean grandiosity.

Elizabeth was no stranger to taking care of others' insecurities and anxieties. She became a pro from an early age, noticing her mother's fears of being alone. Her mother's father died at an early age, and subsequently she was ever vigilant about the slightest rupture in a relationship that might portend the inevitable. And as a result, Elizabeth's mother developed an elaborate set of obsessive-compulsive rituals to make sure that all of her children were within eyesight, physically keeping bathroom doors ajar lest somebody slip away and constantly ruminating about the family member's safety if they so much as went to the local store.

Elizabeth was proficient at taking care of her mother's traumatically informed neuroses and was an easy magnet for her teacher's narcissistic fears as well. Instead of focusing on her own voice, she felt the tension and unexpressed fear and terror of those who were supposed to be mentoring and nurturing her. And this rightfully terrified her now too. Singing became a matter of life or death.

To healthily align her back with her own authority, I said, "I think you are losing connection with your own voice and story, and are getting easily recruited into taking care of your teacher's, just like you had to with your mother. But wait a second—you have the right to have your voice here!"

Encouraging her with both tenderness and fire, I continued, "And it makes total sense why you would be so caring and sensitive to your teacher's needs. Your capacity to really listen and be sensitive to tone is what makes you such a wonderful singer. And yet, we need to also make sure you don't take ownership for what is their tension and not yours!"

She perked up and a little glimmer of chutzpah came out. "Yeah, you're right! I never thought of it like that. I always thought I just had to go along with my teachers and family because I needed them so much. What if you're right? What if they needed *me* more than I thought?"

"That's right. What if you had more strength than you actually knew? What if that's your secret superpower? That's what you deserve to tap into to get your voice back again. And it's yours for the taking!" I smiled as if with a verbal wink, as if to say, "Isn't this great news?"

All of a sudden, I could hear the force and strength come back into her voice, and she began to perk up like a flower that had just found the sun.

Like many clients struggling with losing their voice, we need to not just lend our voice but help them authoritatively get theirs back. Often, we must pluck it out from the mixture of fears, doubts, desires, and wishes they throw at us. They don't mean to throw it at us; it is being jumbled and jostled inside of them, and they are just looking for us to help them sort it out.

That's where therapeutic authority is essential—it separates the essential from the peripheral and helps us tie together even the most seemingly disparate elements. Grayson (2002) rightfully calls it establishing a focal theme, a way of both unpacking and connecting the dominant pattern that forms both the problem and solution of the client's main dilemmas.

Flying and Falling: Losing and Regaining Authority

Susan was an experienced intern at our college counseling center. She worked well with a variety of clients, easily establishing rapport and zeroing in on effective relational strategies for improving the client's anxiety, depression, relationship struggles, social anxiety, and a host of other typical college presentations. But she wasn't fully prepared for Gabby, a silver-tongued premed with a history of a severe eating disorder, cutting, and emotional neglect.

It is not uncommon for clients who present with severe trauma—whether physical, sexual, or emotional abuse or neglect—to take away our sense of therapeutic authority. And while that is how it feels, it's more accurate to say that they require a different kind of therapeutic authority, an emotional and intellectual courage that isn't typically associated with conventional ideas of authority. It is similar to the kind of leadership skill required to engage a community and culture in crisis, manifesting in a much greater capacity for personal self-disclosure and openness to risk.

Because trauma symptoms become protectors as well as persecutors, we must talk down and counter their stubborn resistance, much like a skilled hostage negotiator. Even though the client is often harassed and bothered by their own symptoms, there is an even bigger payoff for the client to rely on them for control and safety. Because of this structural dynamic, we aren't in as much control as the person holding the metaphorical gun to our patient's head. And we have to find an artful and tactful way of appreciating the life-saving qualities of that person holding the gun as well as safeguarding the vulnerable spirit being held and sequestered from the creative world.

Happily, in contrast to the hostage negotiator, our job isn't about seizing the individual and meting out justice but rather bringing them back into the fold of a more integrated multiplicity with open yet responsible arms. Trauma splits off a side of self that becomes an autonomous and possessing presence that kicks out all the other sides, dominates them, and leaves a person with rigid and impersonal forces driving them rather than the humanized sides that they deserve.

An important and discriminating function of therapeutic authority is to help clients uncover and illuminate the multiple meanings of their symptoms, that is, to understand what they are trying to say with their symptoms that they cannot yet say with words. This allows us to help the client find ways of reconnecting to their multiplicity so they can connect more deeply and we can build up a relationship that has more buoyancy to do the emotional work necessary to put this together. Susan helped Gabby delve more deeply and discerningly into the motivations behind her disordered eating.

In associating to her desire for being "bone thin," Gabby acknowledged a wish to be more vulnerable, fragile, and feminine such that there would be no excuse for anybody *not* to take care of her. Gabby had tried in so many other ways and occasions to express her desire for this care, but it was often met with minimization and denial. Her parents, her friends, and even her romantic partner were so often taken in by her seeming intellectual and emotional strength that they forgot about her need for softness and compassion. They would often expect her to put aside her feelings for their immediate attention and often shot back at her when she started to get "needy" with a sarcastic jibe that they imagined would snap her back into the role they knew better. In short, they wouldn't allow her full multiplicity in the room and consequently, Gabby developed an elaborate and entrenched system of defenses to take care of herself.

Gabby described her eating disorder, ED as she liked to

call him, and her cutting as if they were trusted friends: "They take care of me and I take care of them." Her eating disorder was helpful in a backhanded way. It was an unconscious way of regurgitating the problems others were bringing her that she didn't want and expressing her anger at people's monopoliza-tion of her emotional headspace. Most importantly, the starving and purging part of her eating disorder showcased the guilt and undeserving quality she took in as a form of disgust at her own neediness. Gabby looked to her cutting as a badge of honor, the "battle scars of my emotions" that served as reminders of her capacity to carry and conceal her emotions and also as a clever way of rebelling against those who didn't consider her feelings important enough to consider in the first place.

Although Susan felt more confident as she found ways to understand and zero in on the potential meanings of Gabby's confusing behavior, it rubbed her the wrong when Gabby talked about a desire to be more feminine. As a lesbian woman, she felt the term was too gendered, problematic, and potentially oppressive, and it kicked up a loaded constellation of painful memories for her.

It became important for Susan to be able to process this in supervision more freely with me, and find a new, common language with Gabby to express the fragility, vulnerability, and delicacy that she was longing to have supported. In addition, this allowed Susan to more deeply explore and process her own wounds at not being supported as a lesbian woman, and more generally in her own family story as one who had been stereo-typed herself for not being feminine enough.

It was very easy for Susan's s authority to feel undermined and sabotaged. After a particularly tender and close moment one week when Gabby finally let her guard down and stopped using her consistent sarcasm, Gabby came to the next meeting to boast with glee that she had cut herself and did so very deeply after session. It was clear that Gabby needed to feel a sense of control and that her disdain for her own neediness was taking aim at Susan.

In supervision, Susan and I developed a metaphor to help make sense of the scary and unpredictable feeling of working with Gabby and to regain her therapeutic authority. We used a metaphor of a trapeze act or high-wire tightrope, envisioning Gabby's steps outside her symptoms as learning to balance and leap despite fears. At times, Susan functioned as the safety net underneath the metaphorical trapeze, providing a stable and solid holding environment within which Gabby could practice her new skills and fall if needed. But more often, the dynamic felt more akin to a joint trapeze act in which Susan first demonstrated the move that they could then practice back and forth.

Not surprisingly, this part of the metaphor captured the stress, fear, and danger that Susan felt in working with Gabby, and underscored the bravery that it took to be able to hold on to her authority. This greatly helped Susan to normalize her fear and contextualize within the sphere of doing something rather heroic, and mirroring the heroic work that Gabby would be undertaking in healing her trauma. The metaphor also functioned as a creative way of translating Gabby symptoms in a new, more adaptive relational dynamic, a way to build up a more flexible and supportive intrapsychic structure.

More Authority to Give

With some clients, you'll feel like you don't know if you can give them any more authority since they already seem to have so much. Maybe they function fairly well in their work or in their relationships, or they are good patients, so to speak, so why push them? Often, if you look closer, there'll be more good stuff, and that's where the creative action is.

Matt was one of these clients. He always had a voracious appetite for working and playing hard, and as a typical introverted extrovert, he also needed equal doses of alone and social time. A biologist by day and bartender by night, Matt excelled at an unusual mix that made most people question him: who was he really? Like a tug of war, extroverted friends wanted him to declare himself as one of their own, as his more introverted lab mates tried to convince him that his hours committed to solitary research were a telltale sign of his membership in their tribe.

Matt was accustomed to this pull on even deeper levels. He had come to New York from Ohio and often felt out of place living and working in fast-paced Manhattan, but was also intrigued by the challenge of harnessing its raw energy. He was often scolded by his Bible Belt parents for his intense focus on the secular scientific world of the biotech company where he worked, not to mention their chagrin at his weekend job as a bartender. Matt felt like he had lived in two worlds but could never quite join them.

My supervisee David was completely baffled as to how to help him. By all accounts, Matt was doing pretty well. He landed a fulfilling and lucrative job in his field of choice, healthily separated and individuated from his family of origin, and was set to launch into an exciting new life in the big city. What more could David give him?

We explored the value of helping Matt own and consolidate the dual citizenship that he had both in the introverted and extroverted worlds and the secular and religious worlds. And with an analogy to the third eye chakra, we could help him to see that it afforded him much fuller vision and wisdom than others and offered him a special superpower that enabled him not only to see both sides but many shades of gray in between.

At the same time, we also talked about the inner and outer conflicts he so often felt—those tugs of war—both inside and outside of his family that we could now represent more fully as this creative growing process. Matt was able to see the ways he had to maintain loyalty to his home and family on the one hand, and the adventure and opportunity, represented by the city, science, and his extroverted side too.

Another exciting opportunity for David was to see that he didn't have to help Matt take on his authority in the conventional way by growing up but rather to help him become more emotionally curious about growing down. He could add more depth and nuance to Matt's life by helping him to more deeply and clearly express the frustration, ambivalence, and resentment of growing up in a world that only honored one side most fully.

In order to make it more dramatic and to capture Matt's playful wit, David analogized a part of their work as deprogramming. He had Matt envision his parents as a set of characters from the television series *The Americans*, a family of Russian spies going through all of the motions of living as if American while simultaneously loyal to a whole different set of rules.

Matt was smitten with this new analogy as it helped more easily crystallize something he had always felt but couldn't put easily into words. How could he? His parents were supportive, hardworking, and loving people, and he could never muster the rhyme nor reason to question them, not to mention in such a dramatic way as David had offered.

By working this metaphor, Matt was able to realize how alone he had been all his life in feeling this "secret" and how important it was for him to have his therapist as a new ally in joining these worlds. He was also amazed to recognize the synchronicity of his job move as more than just a financial and geographic shift. It finally dawned on Matt that the true reason he took the job in the first place was the mentor and boss he would be working for, a Russian émigré who himself had learned how to bridge both the extroverted and introverted worlds and the secular and religious worlds Matt too longed to bridge. Without realizing it, Matt had found his lifelong mentor and new authority to help him foster his own. And little did David know that he was a central part of this new mission too.

Therapist Responsiveness Revisited: Integrating Therapeutic Authority and Presence

Just as we noted in Chapter 4 that therapist responsiveness is dependent on an attuned and dynamic therapeutic presence, so too is it based in command of one's therapeutic authority, the capacity to focus one's interventions in a way that is most effective for the individual client sitting before you. Levenson (2021) sums it up best: "Therapist responsiveness is doing the right thing in the right way with the right person at the right time."

Just as the right brain needs the left brain to focus it, find the right words, and take active deliberate steps, as therapists we rely on our therapeutic authority to give shape to new changes and execute the interventions that transform our client's lives. When we unite therapeutic presence and therapeutic authority, we own a responsive therapeutic voice that invites, courts, and fosters the emerging voice of our clients in the creative improvisation that is psychotherapy.

To put it in better context, notice how when we teach basic counseling skills we start first with rapport building, reflective listening, and all of the other humanistic, existential, and dynamic techniques for tuning in, listening deeply, and making sense of what is at the core of one's emotional and cognitive interests and conflicts. Therapeutic presence, as our reliable right-brain-to-right-brain connection, enables us to set the foundation for a deeper alliance and foundation for beginning to tinker more fully.

And it's because the right brain is the master, connected even more deeply to our instinctive, sensory, and body-based centers. It is our conductor as emotion-regulation musicians, with each of us playing both the prepared and improvisatory scores of ourselves, our relationships, and the world. Once we attend to that, we are free to inquire into and execute the left-brain higher-order decisions, the mind-based discriminating and focused ways in which we select and make moves in our relationships in the infinite chess game of life. The left brain showcases us as idea- and thought-generating creatures, our phenomenal ability to zero in, predict, and reason our way out of predicaments and into greater possibilities.

As in the case of Todd above, it is fairly organic to have these sides integrate, synergize, and collaborate, and this is what accounts for the tremendous power of psychotherapy. It compounds the wisdom, depth, and nuance of the right and left brain and opens up myriad opportunities for creative witnessing and new storytelling, both of which enable a much richer and fuller musical appreciation of our lives.

As we've noted throughout these pages, it is a right-brain, left-brain, right-brain process. Like a three-step dance, once we get in the habit of noticing how we can attend to and work with these sides, there is no stopping how much opens up for us, as in the first case illustration of therapeutic improvisation in this book, the struggling jazz pianist. Why is it that we always come up with so many new things?

It might be more apt to say why do we always come up with so many new things about seemingly old things, and in so many unexpectedly interesting ways? Because that's how we're built, and that's what therapy helps us accomplish: to capitalize, optimize, and embrace most fully what is most humanly possible, intriguing, maddening, and, yes, possible, echoing Donald Winnicott (2016), in the story we are both making and discovering at every turn.

Whether we are using humanistic, dynamic, cognitive-behavioral, gestalt, or any other school of therapy, we are well advised to note the ways in which we go back and forth from the foundation of right-brain presence to the implementation of left-brain therapeutic authority, no matter what our metatheoretical orientation. In fact, one might even go so far as to say that in the history of psychotherapy itself, we have seen a continual wrestling between the right-brain and left-brain aspects of various theoretical orientations, a curious and humorously human way of grappling with our essential structure: the constant oscillating and reconciliation of our two brains.

To use broad brushstrokes, we witnessed the right-brain, body-based, evenly hovering attention origins of Freud's revolutionary psychoanalysis being supplanted by its own overly dogmatic left-brain interpretation-driven mode of classical analysis. This was tempered and corrected by a more left-brained behaviorist project meant to move away from the immeasurable and unpredictable, and was later tempered by a right-brained humanistic mission of coming back to our right-brained basics of listening and tuning in to therapeutic presence. We even saw the evolution of psychoanalysis attempting to correct its left-leaning tendencies with the interpersonal tradition that now forms the basis of interpersonal neurobiology.

We've seen the continual back and forth again with the advent of second-wave cognitive-behavioral approaches, attempting to better mobilize the power of the left brain in tempering the distortions of the right-brain-based emotional world. And these in turn were later balanced by third-wave therapies such as dialectical behavior therapy and acceptance commitment therapy that brought back mindfully based right-brain-friendly body techniques, and similarly we've seen a renaissance of other body-based modalities seeking to bring the right brain back as the master and the left brain as its trusted emissary. And it seems like we will continue to see this pattern.

In many ways, it is a perpetual cycle of reckoning with our fundamental biological and psychological structure. As McGilchrist (2009) notes, it is the perpetual struggle and complementarity of the right and left brain that begets the fundamentally unique human project and promise. On the micro as well as macro levels, we are witness to the fundamental ways in which the science of our interpersonal neurobiology shapes, contains, and expresses the artistry of our lives and of therapy itself.

EXERCISE 1: Am I Self-Doubting or Overzealous in My Therapeutic Authority?

It's pretty common to lean in one direction or the other here. As the old Spiderman saying goes, with great power comes great responsibility. Most of us are either eager to enjoy this power or shy away from its bigness.

WHY AM I SO OVERZEALOUS IN MY AUTHORITY?

If you are overzealous in your authority, might you be running away from or avoiding feelings of being out of control?

Might you be shying away from your therapeutic presence, from allowing yourself to more deeply steep in not fully knowing yet or in the emotions of the moment?

Are there ways in which you are scared of sharing your power with your clients?

Let's take some pressure off you to go so fast. You can still be in healthy power and control without having to command it. Your patient will still respect and value you, and you can be on the lookout for ways in which they can join in on sharing the authority together. More often than not, clients are hazily if not sharply aware of what their areas of concern are and their wishes to make it better. They are looking for us to temporarily take on authority to help us regain theirs, but we don't have to shoulder it all. Remember this as you explore, investigate, and intervene with them.

Sometimes, you might play your client's defense attorney in countering a very critical or maladaptive side of self, and you need that authority to help them. At other times, you might be their cheerleader and encourager to help them find the voice that they need to bring back online into the conversation.

Will often felt he needed to be continually moving the session in the direction it needed to go, like an athlete on the basketball court needing to constantly dribble the ball. He had grown up with a lot of pressure to be decisive and active, and as a high achiever this facet was only reinforced further. We worked on allowing plays to get set up more naturally, recognizing that therapy, unlike competitive sports, wasn't adversarial but collaborative. By learning how to share the power of setting the pace and direction, Will found that his clients could surprise him by showing him plays he didn't realize were possible on the court. Not only did this energize him, it relaxed him and allowed him to see the unexpected joy of allowing feelings and thoughts to take their own time to emerge. As he felt more comfortable with this new skill, he joked that it was a lot like how he felt when he sat up in the nosebleed seats at basketball games. Although at first he hated that he wasn't right up in the action on the floor, he could more easily watch the plays take form from a distance.

WHY AM I SO SCARED OF MY AUTHORITY?

If you are self-doubting in your authority, are you concerned about the problematic and potential destructive uses of your power as a therapist? Have you witnessed potentially problematic or destructive uses of power in your own personal life, and are you trying to overcompensate for it by not fully taking on your own power?

If you come from a socially marginalized group, are you feeling a shadow concern about becoming an oppressor rather than a facilitator? How can you realign your power as a joint and mutual sharing of power?

Leila worked from a feminist relational approach and was ever sensitive to the ways in which oppressive systems could silence and disempower her clients, especially the many young women with whom she worked. At times, even though she had very clear, interesting, and relevant observations to share with her clients, she held them back for fear of "mansplaining." In our work together, we found a way for Leila to continue to respect and hold open a space for her clients at the same time that she could value and share her own opinion. In fact, we reframed this as a way to more deeply practice and model her feminist perspective to her clients, allowing it to truly showcase the equality, mutuality, and dignity that she so valued in this approach.

Overall, therapeutic authority can be as enjoyable as being a bandleader who is both the maestro and yet ever attentive to getting everyone in the band featured and collaborating in the mutual fun of the music together.

EXERCISE 2: Deliberate Practice

Building on the science of expertise of Anders Ericsson (2016), Tony Rousmaniere (2016) and Hanna Levenson (2021) speak and write about the importance of deliberate practice, the conscious method of strengthening areas that are less developed but are crucial to being a solidly integrated and authoritative therapist. Deliberate practice requires you to practice outside your comfort zone beyond your current abilities in service of successive refinement and improved performance on the therapeutic stage. Chow, Miller, et al. (2015) found that neither age, gender, degree, experience, supervision, workshops, books read, nor theoretical orientation predicted highly effective therapists. Instead, it was the solo time spent in deliberate practice that truly made the difference.

Playing off the 10,000-hour rule, the idea here is to identify and then practice the skills that don't come as naturally or easily for you. It could be making an empathic statement when you are finding a behavior maladaptive, self-destructive, or unsavory. It might be interrupting overly indulgent complaining that avoids therapeutic work, helping the client become more active in trying a new strategy to tackle their difficult issues. Or it could be working on the balancing act of any number of therapeutic microskills that need tweaking: identifying subtle shades of unexpressed affect, articulating underlying schemas or cognitive distortions, or pointing out maladaptive behaviors in a nonshaming and constructive manner, to name just a few.

A supervisee named Jessica was amazing at developing a solid rapport, but she got completely tongue-tied and fearful when she had to do risk assessment and crisis intervention. Together, we formulated scripts she could practice that fit better with her compassionate, relational approach, such as, "I know this is a difficult question to answer. I also know that for a lot of people who are feeling so depressed, it's not uncommon to have thoughts of killing oneself. Has that ever happened for you recently during this difficult time?" With deliberate practice, we constructed statements like this to help her refine her confidence and expand her clinical repertoire so she could be ready and comfortable in the improvisational performance that is crisis work.

Levenson (2021) offers up a 1–10 scale to locate where on

the practice level this skill is for you so that you can better gauge your current comfort and confidence and notice your progress as you work deliberately on the skill itself. She also shows how you can work in tandem with good supervision to model and practice these discrete skills we all need in our tool kit to feel and become more authoritative in our roles.

She challenges us to look at our schedules and think about our most difficult, feared, or otherwise stress-inducing clients, and locate what are the microskills and interventions that they are leading us to strengthen. Again, it's crucial to frame this as a creative building exercise rather than an exercise in taking your inventory of deficits. Remember the Critic we discussed in the introduction—make sure that part of you doesn't commandeer this exercise. Instead, allow this to be informed by what Carol Dweck (2008) defines as a growth mindset opportunity, the capacity to be open and excited about the dynamic process of learning anew and adding to the creative work of being a therapist. Just as any good writer learns to love and appreciate the process of writing, so to must we as clinicians embrace the continual revising process of working on those persnickety personal and professional stumbling blocks.

The best meta-part about this exercise is that it reminds us that like athletes, we are always trying to up our game in different and difficult conditions. Like a golfer who learns how to make shots from the rough or in the sand trap or how to read very tricky greens, this regular and deliberate practice will help you become more and more confident in your improvisational skills to deal with anything a client throws at you.

6

WHY YOU NEED
LATERAL MENTORS TOO

How Did We Get Here and Where Are We Going?

It might seem strange to talk about mentors at this point. Haven't we figured out your therapeutic voice well enough, equipped with presence and authority, so that mentors become obsolete? Yes and no. As we'll see, both traditional and lateral mentors support and accelerate the development of your voice and your continued creative growth as a clinician.

Our journey to a therapeutic voice like an artistic voice is to continue consulting and conversing with the masters as well as our contemporaries. Our goal is to amalgamate our many formative influences and at the same time create new opportunities for creative collaborations with our colleagues. A continual inner and outer dialogue, this stance keeps us constantly learning, tinkering, and revitalizing our creative muse.

I've heard of traditional mentors—like Hayden to Beethoven or Rodin to Rilke—but what is a lateral mentor? Think of it like a good musician who gets intrigued about working not only within their musical lane but also collaborating with folks way outside their own genre. Think Johnny Cash and Nine Inch Nails, Tony Bennett and Lady Gaga, Yo-Yo Ma and Bobby McFerrin, Elvis Costello and Anne Sofie von Otter, and Alicia Keys and Jay-Z. With this synergy, we become even more effective, creative, and transformative in our work with our clients and, even better, we pave the way for a continually regenerating work and life balance.

The Power of Traditional Mentors

Three Little Engines author and TEDx speaker Bob McKinnon shows us the power of traditional mentors with a simple twist. Confessing to the TEDx audience that he knows the cardinal rule of PowerPoint slides is to have no more than six words, he proceeds to display a slide crowded with names upon names, text upon text. As a PowerPoint slide, it is all wrong, but as an illustration of the power of mentoring, it is totally right.

Without his great-grandfather making the hard voyage to America, his mother as a buffer against the abuse and troubled environment around him, or even people he didn't know, like the originator of *Sesame Street* and the inventor of the Pell Grant, McKinnon muses that his story would not truly be possible. As he declares, "This is my dream team. This is how I got here. If you take any one name off there, I'm not here."

These are the many and varied known and inadvertent mentors we collect along the way, the teachers who inspire and encourage us, the parents who see promise in us, and, if we are lucky, the supervisors that help us apprentice in this rich field. We are most familiar with the traditional mentors, the hierarchical mentors who are typically older, wiser, and more experienced. They provide us with a vision of how we can put things together, and we are inspired by their model.

Who were the family members, teachers (academic, music, dance, etc.), sports coaches, camp counselors, heroes of your imagination from books, movies, music, and supervisors who inspired you? I can think of two very special traditional mentors in my life who made an indelible mark on my growth and development. Like the Molière character who is surprised to learn that he has been speaking prose all his life without knowing it, these mentors taught me how to find my therapeutic voice before I even knew there was such a concept altogether.

When I was a boy, my mother and I had weekly "fireside chats." A social worker and student of literature, she'd inquire about the latest books I was reading—*To Kill a Mockingbird, The Glass Menagerie, The Bridge of San Luis Rey, Othello*, and the Bible itself—and together we'd find ways of connecting them to the general trials and tribulations of becoming more fully human. These books became my good friends, guides, and companions, and I learned from them and from my mother to love, as Rilke said, the questions themselves.

I was taught to always be curious about what new idea, feeling, or form I could find in what I already thought I knew and, most importantly, that talking itself was the magic that allowed this hidden art to emerge. My mother encouraged me to be on the lookout for this wonder everywhere—when talking or writing about my own hopes and fears, speaking to a friend or waitress at the local diner, people watching from afar, and experiencing great art. Unbeknownst to me, it was this enthusiasm, mentoring, and poetic sensibility that brought me to the door of psychology.

Not surprisingly, my mother also instinctively modeled for me the combination of therapeutic presence and authority I would later come to discover on my own. As a teenager, I would often go to her as a sounding board on some challenge I was having in school, in a friendship, or in a relationship. Many times, I can distinctly recall her listening intently, and nudging my story along. Looking back on it now, it wasn't so much a verbal prodding in that classic Rogerian way as a nonverbal, right-brained feeling that there was a palpably open space and profound and open attention—an embodied, benevolent, and warm presence—there for me to let myself surrender into my own process.

I would always be stunned when, after a long stretch, all my mother needed to say was a few words of some new observation that we felt forming in the story itself, and just as often as she did, I was quick to riff on it too and make the connections to all that had come before, and start playing delightedly with this new improvisation we had found together.

As in our model of a therapeutic voice, my mother was a very sensitive and patient listener, showing an open-minded, permissive, and kind presence that made it easy to unfold and freely associate and wander in and out of much-needed emotional and intellectual territory. At the same time, I was also amazed at how this very mild-mannered and sensitive person could move confidently to the core of the issue in a surge of virtuosic beauty. Her well-timed and nuanced summation— which came across not as commanding but inspiring—had a way of making me feel like she had fully seen not just the me I knew but the me I was becoming in process, and I would feel revitalized and more self-assured in zeroing in on the heart of the matter too.

A mother is one of the first and most important teachers of interpersonal neurobiology, giving among the warmest and most enduring lessons in the improvisatory music of right-brain-to-right-brain connection, showcasing the science and art of interpersonal closeness, compromise, and creativity. Carl Jung (1933) said that mother-love was "the mysterious root of all growth and change; the love that means homecoming, shelter, and the long silence from which everything begins and in which everything ends."

Starting from this home and secure base, to echo both Donald Winnicott and Mary Ainsworth, these lessons are elaborated and refined through the improvisatory dance we continue with everyone else: fathers, siblings, teachers, friends, romantic partners, colleagues, and clients. The empirical observations into our own inner world in concert with learning about the mysterious and intriguing complexity of others becomes the diamond through which we see ourselves and the magical scintillation that animates us all.

Another unexpected mentor for my work as a therapist came in the form of my piano teacher. A Juilliard-trained concert pianist and composer, Avraham Sternklar had the capacity to outplay, outthink, and outmatch anybody who came into his home studio, a suburban living room dwarfed by back-to-back concert grand pianos and a personalized gallery of his wife's oil paintings.

But instead of finding a tortured genius, an emotionally unpredictable diva, I was impressed by his unique capacity to blend a rigorous, disciplined, and sharp intellect with a warm, inviting, and flexible emotional availability. Before I even knew the terms, Mr. Sternklar was showing me how to blend therapeutic presence and authority, a capacity to listen deeply and curiously and to be discriminating and commanding all at once.

How did he model this? When working on a difficult piece, Sternklar would reassure me that the dilemmas I was facing—whether in finding the right piano fingering, coordinating hands, being attentive to incorporating dynamics, or crafting a beautiful musical line—was something that even he and the masters struggled with too. Making me feel a part of the club, he went a step further by playfully showing me how we might make it a new game together to work on this interesting dilemma and unexpected magic trick we were all hoping to pull off. I was always tickled by how the 5-year-olds and 15-year-olds at the annual recital would be treated with the same respect, consideration, and applause, a reflection of Mr. Sternklar's ethos that we are all masters, no matter how big or small.

Sternklar also did something else extraordinary. Like Michelangelo seeing the fully realized sculpture within the unhewn block of marble, he could see the potential in me and his other students, and he spoke to it and took pride in it as deeply as he did the sides that felt clunky and as yet unrealized. He held the optimism, courage, and hope that I could take on more than I believed I could at the moment, whether playing a Mozart piano concerto, a Bach fugue, a Brahms intermezzo, or anything else I couldn't imagine before. It was his support and love in his presence and authority that spurred it all on.

My piano teacher also had a knack for showcasing how we could put many disparate parts—melody, harmony, and line—together to make a beautiful performance. And he also could use his discriminating left-brain capacity to analyze and showcase the hidden musical architecture that made a piece of music work. An extraordinary embodiment of fully developed logic and feeling, Mr. Sternklar taught so much more than piano, and as you'll find, most of our greatest mentors teach us something that goes far above and beyond the discipline they seem to be teaching us. Who knew a music teacher would teach me so much about psychology and about myself?

I can flash back to my 11th grade English teacher, George Blouin, who read and acted out loud *Macbeth*, *Lord of the Flies*, and *Brave New World*, showcasing the true beauty and power of "words as X-rays." I remember my social studies teacher, Loretta Kriaris, who showed the miraculous sweep of history and the revolutionary story of American democracy and the reach of an enhanced vocabulary with words like "commensurate" and "invidious." That is just the tip of the iceberg of all the mentors that would appear on my PowerPoint slide. Think back now about the 5, 10, 15, 20, or many, many more people you'd have on your own PowerPoint slide of mentors who helped you become more fully who you are.

Upping Your Game: The Power of Lateral Mentors

Developmental psychologist Debbie Heiser (2020) introduced me to the concept of lateral mentors with the story of two Steves. Steve J. was working for Atari and was on a very tight deadline for a new game that could outwit the competition. He couldn't crack the case on how to smooth out the technological issues to make the game really go and, racking his brain, he surrendered to his own temporary limits. But he didn't give up.

He consulted with his buddy Steve W. and managed to get him to drive over after a long day's work at Hewlett Packard to tinker with it. The game that emerged—Breakout—was the beginning of a long-term creative relationship that saw Steve Jobs and Steve Wozniak revolutionize computing as we know it.

Lateral mentors are the engine of the digital revolution and have recalibrated our largely left-brain model of professional development. They remind us that to find our mentors, we need to look not only up but sideways, sometimes in another department, discipline, or field, for the creative spark we need to get our work humming again.

What is even better is that when we recognize these folks, we will also find our way to give back to them too, collaborating in unexpected ways, and developing the kind of generativity that Erik Erikson (Erikson & Coles, 2000) said brings out our undeniably human drive to contribute to the world and generations to come.

Ironically, my own lateral mentor came in the form of none

other than the researcher of lateral mentors herself. I found Debbie Heiser on LinkedIn and was intrigued by the speaking and writing she was doing as a psychologist and wanted to learn more. As I looked closer at her profile, I realized we had gone to the same graduate program at the exact same time but were in parallel tracks. As clinical and developmental psychology students, we had been in some classes together but didn't connect until some 15 years later.

What quickly emerged was a lateral mentoring field day. Debbie quickly zoomed in on ways to help me find and secure speaking gigs and immediately set me up with colleagues she knew that hosted podcasts as a way of improving my speaking chops. She became an encouraging sounding board on several book ideas I was batting around that needed practical help and support from a knowledgeable colleague. She supported the wisdom and originality of my clinical ideas and focused on possible homes and venues to put them out into the world. While not in my wheelhouse, Debbie was quick on the draw with finding concrete solutions, practical strategies, and networking connections that could solve my problems. You could say she was my Steve Wozniak.

Before long, lateral mentors quickly develop a mutual and collaborative give and take, and soon enough, in our first phone call, I learned that Debbie was intrigued by my TEDx experience and curious about how to do one herself. Here's where my moment of paying her back was ready to come online.

After hearing her work on mentors, I knew she had a powerful TED talk in her and was sure I could help her put an idea together to apply. But I could also sense that she needed some encouragement and confidence to feel worthy and really make her talk sing. Just as she had lent me the solutions I needed for my dilemma, I helped her see the poetry and drama in her ideas. Months later, when I was helping her craft and practice the talk, like a stage director, I lent her my artistic chutzpah so she could take on a more edgy and humorous tone in her talk, saying, "I love the professor from Iowa who is kind and smart, but I want to hear the funny and passionate Debbie I laugh with on the phone. Let's try that story again and give it a little bit more of that umph!"

By the time Debbie was ready to go onstage, she was virtually doing stand-up and had all of the lines she was nervous about handily memorized. But our lateral mentorship didn't stop there. As for Jobs and Wozniak, it was just the beginning.

A Lateral Approach to Work-Life Balance

Lateral mentors are the lifeblood of our creative work. They inspire, encourage, problem solve, brainstorm, cheerlead, and defend us in times of both promise and struggle. And without us even realizing it, their interpersonal support provides us with the kind of regular energy that keeps our work and personal life balanced.

We don't talk much about the crucial aspect of social support and emotional connection that our work lives bring to us, but they do. Before the digital revolution, there was a more left-brain-centered approach to work focused on achievement, success, and a linear progression up the ladder. But now, perhaps because of the way in which the right brain has become more crucial—as Daniel Pink (2006) noted, it will "rule the future"—we are much more aware of and tuned in to the deeper value of creative, emotional, and aesthetic fulfillment.

I have a favorite uncle who has always reminded me to make sure that whatever I do brings lots of "psychic income." In other words, make sure that you don't just gather expertise and become useful but enjoy your work thoroughly and let it recharge your personal life as it does your professional life. The work-from-anywhere movement, spurred further by the demands of a global pandemic, has only further amplified this need for greater integration and balance of our work and home life. And yet as attentive improvisational therapists, we are ever tuned in to the parallel and intersecting worlds of our professional artistry and personal well-being. In fact, as we've discussed, in this work of developing a voice we learn to become more fully responsive, not only to our clients but even more to ourselves. And that, as Robert Frost said, can make all the difference.

Developing a Network of Lateral Mentors

There are many ways to find and connect with lateral mentors. Throughout my graduate school and early career days, I'd head over to the William Alanson White Institute for their monthly lectures as if it were a jazz club to listen to veteran players and up-and-coming clinicians. Whether it was Philip Bromberg, Edgar Levenson, Nancy McWilliams, Marilyn Charles, or a variety of other clinical titans I had long admired or young therapists and writers I had never heard of before, I began to see how all of them became my new lateral mentors.

Their clinical work and ideas would stimulate and dialogue with my own. I would ask the speakers—many of whom were my heroes—questions both during and after their formal presentations and write down notes, not only about their material but also those ideas that informed the riffs and licks that I wanted to play as well. Lateral mentors enable us to have an internal and external conversation that enlarges us in ways we often can't initially see or measure. Like retirement savings, the benefits of lateral mentors quickly compound and accrue.

Going to talks also became a springboard for chatting with

those sitting next to me. Through these inspired conversations, fellow attendees quickly become new colleagues and possible collaborators. I'm sure you have noticed the buzz and energy you get from going to a great conference, and how wonderful it is to meet so many like-minded and interesting people ever on the search for deepening our craft. It is very often those places where we find the kinds of unexpected lateral mentors we need to up our game. And even better, many of these folks we meet at conferences become more than just our colleagues—they become our friends.

I first met psychologists and authors Chris Willard and Mitch Abblett at the *Psychotherapy Networker* Symposium. They were giving a workshop about how therapists can get published. Throughout the Q & A, I could tell that our ideas about therapy, creativity, and writing were very sympatico, and I could see the feeling was mutual. Chris, Mitch, and I kept in touch and over time what emerged was a joint idea to create a community of psychologist-writers to support each other in the process of writing, doing therapy, and managing work-life balance. We started our group in the midst of the COVID-19 pandemic, and it became not only a laboratory of book ideas and clinical supervision but also a community and support group as therapists, writers, and parents in the midst of a collective trauma. Unwittingly, we had set up a family-style network of lateral mentors that could support both our professional dreams and aspirations, through the many unexpected storms of a world under siege.

The beauty of lateral mentorship is that it takes all of our many influences—even our traditional mentors—and brings them on an equal playing field, making it about ways in which we can support each other together. Just as we do in our sessions with clients, we are always striving to develop this mutual and creative interplay. This is the essence of therapeutic improvisation.

Therapeutic improvisation respects and invites the authority and presence of the other to intermingle with our own. In this process, we support and develop our own artistic and personal voice alongside those of our clients and colleagues. In so doing, we make even more intriguing polyphony, a music that transcends the beauty of our solitary multiplicities.

Internal Lateral Mentors

As we develop lateral mentors on the outside, so too do we build them on the inside. We often forget and downplay the side gigs we have had and their special power in helping us in our therapeutic work. But as it turns out, these seemingly peripheral and disconnected aspects of our career and personal lives often become the internal lateral mentors we need to turbocharge our clinical growth. Whether it is your prior work or experience as an athlete, dancer, musician, writer, businessperson, magician, actor, or any other seemingly unrelated field, these experiences can help you just as fully as any flesh-and-blood mentor.

Todd, from Chapters 3 and 5, started his career in sales and marketing. As we talked in supervision about the way he approached therapy, we leaned into how he had honed his chops from learning how to notice what a customer really needs and wants, and being able to find an approach point to help them make the right choice. It was no wonder that Todd could think quickly on his feet about a particular question or intervention that could help his client achieve buy-in for the direction he was trying to move the therapy. Unbeknownst to Todd, he had been practicing it way before he even set foot in graduate school.

Michelle was amazed to find that her experience as an actress helped her immeasurably as a therapist. Like a good actor, she could deeply dig into her clients' motivations and fully inhabit their emotional world as if it were her own, and, better yet, she had an uncanny knack for making improvisational adjustments as if her speaking partner had hit or flubbed her line. It didn't matter because she was prepared for both.

Being a good therapist, she told me, is like being a triple threat. You're an actor who has the courage to show up and delve into your vulnerability, a singer who can find your pitch and listen and blend well with the ensemble, and a dancer who knows how important it is to be connected to the movements below your neck.

Lifelong Creativity

The lateral and traditional mentors in our lives form an intricate and powerful matrix of continual inspiration, fulfillment, and support. They provide us with the sustainable energy we need inside and out to fully realize our therapeutic voice, and they nurture and hone the improvisational skills we continue to master as we develop the music of our work as therapists.

EXERCISE 1: Who's on Your PowerPoint?

All young artists seek models in their apprentice years,
models whose style, technical mastery, and innovations
can teach them. Young painters may haunt the galleries
of the Met or the Louvre; young composers may go to
concerts or study scores. All art, in this sense, starts out as
"derivative," highly influenced by, if not a direct imitation
or paraphrase of, the admired and emulated models.

—Oliver Sacks, *The Creative Self*

Imagine yourself putting together a PowerPoint slide of all the important mentors you have had in your life. Who are the teachers, coaches, family members, supervisors, authors, role models, heroes from your imagination in books, music, movies, and pop culture, and any other influences in your life who have inspired and guided you?

What are the strengths and gifts you have witnessed in them, and how have you imitated and incorporated them yourself?

How can you take in these positive qualities from mentors outside of your field (music teachers, sports coaches, dance instructors, work bosses, etc.) into your ongoing creative therapeutic work?

Who are the internal lateral mentors from your side gigs, and how can you make them more of an ongoing and deliberate part of your therapeutic work?

EXERCISE 2: Your Extended Community of Lateral Mentors

Who are the lateral mentors in your world, and in what ways do you love collaborating together?

Who are the lateral mentors you have met at conferences, on LinkedIn, on Instagram, Facebook groups, and so on?

Are there people you forget are lateral mentors because you didn't have the category before?

TOWARD A NEW VISION
OF MENTAL HEALTH

Constantly my patients drive me to question, and
constantly my questions drive me to patients.
—Oliver Sacks, *The Man Who Mistook His Wife for a Hat*

Music is liquid architecture; architecture is frozen music.
—Johann Wolfgang von Goethe

My Problem With Problems

I've always had a *problem* with those who just see *problems*. To be more precise, it's the way we casually throw that word around and how much it drips with the subtext of inferiority. The word's etymology is much kinder and more curious, denoting a question or riddle that is thrown before us or the barrier that interferes with our forward movement. It's those kinds of problems I'm intrigued by and just fascinated with; they're the ones that generate creative momentum, that invite us to make our way together through the labyrinth.

Our system of mental health tends toward cataloging and categorizing the many varieties of our clients' psychological problems, but it is less inclined to draw attention to an essential feature of our human condition: our capacity for creativity. We are very quick to forget and surrender our creativity and mistakenly believe it is only the province of artists. And even artists themselves—writers, musicians, actors, dancers, and painters—mistakenly sequester their artistic powers from their personal lives. It is a fundamental mistake on our part as individuals and as a collective, and most importantly as a field, to jettison these riches.

While we have so often marveled at the frozen music of our architecture—our discrete systems of classification, treatment interventions, or even our single-minded devotion to our role as therapist—we easily forget the multifaceted, dynamic, and ever-shifting music of our work. So often this is because we have neglected to factor in our multiplicity, the alarming and maddening complementarity and contradiction we are each built with that provides the necessary tension, dissonance, and spark to keep our fluid natures happily in motion. In short, we forget how to live a life of psychological creativity and improvisation.

We bring this creativity out through our therapeutic voice. Our voice encourages, inspires, and activates our patient's voices and simultaneously energizes and strengthens our own; it provides the circular flow of mutuality that is essential to the creative process of improvisation. And as we have seen, we do this by effectively integrating the right- and left-brain features of therapeutic presence and authority.

It is a responsiveness and creativity that goes both ways. Therapeutic presence is, for our patients and for ourselves, a specialized listening that we cultivate to sensitively tune in to the moment-to-moment adjustments we need to make in order to be in sync with our ever-shifting multiplicities. Therapeutic authority is the confidence and competence to pinpoint and express the multiplicity in our patients just as it is a sharper and more refined understanding of our multidimensional experience with them. In short, both become the features of a responsive and improvisational art that we nurture, cultivate, and enjoy together. The mismatches and ruptures in our relationship and in their internal ones—the tests, struggles, and confusing symptoms of anxiety, depression, and social disconnection—are the necessary dissonances of working this music.

Psychotherapy outcome researcher Jeanne C. Watson (2021) rightly talks about an essential quality for all creative therapists: quick access to varied ways of verbally representing experiences and the capacity to "break set swiftly." Like the improvisational musician, actor, comedian, or dancer, the improvisational therapist can form and synthesize the big picture and the details while simultaneously being able to just as easily let them go to allow other new forms to emerge in the moment. As Watson concludes, "This quicksilver, malleable way of interacting while remaining grounded and centered, may be the essence of being responsive in psychotherapy."

The Tune We All Have to Play

At the close of a very illuminating and productive session one afternoon with Ben (Chapter 4), fascinated by the depth and breadth of the psyche's capacity to express its own brilliance, I was talking about how silly it was that we weren't all taught about the harmonic changes he knew inside and out as a musician. "Isn't it a shame," I said, "we aren't all taught how to read the changes of the psyche?" And without missing a beat, he responded, "Yeah, it's *the* tune we all have to play!"

An accomplished jazz vocalist, Cathy was regularly amazed at how we would find ways of capturing the many different changes she was internally experiencing, from her family drama to her romantic relationships to her identity as a female jazz artist in what so often felt like a boy's club. One day we talked in depth about the double standards she felt as a woman being objectified for her weight and appearance, and it linked back to an early experience of being exploited by an older man she had thought might show her the value and recognition she had always been craving from her father.

She juxtaposed this experience with her more mutual, equal, and nuanced relationship with her current boyfriend ("he drinks his 'respect women' juice") and her own renewed desire to lose weight for herself. As we explored this, she began to take back the unconscious layers of protection she carried to shield herself from the injustices and traumas of a male world that had not found a way to integrate her female worth, power, and beauty. And we both thought it was no accident and quite poetic that this topic came to our attention on International Women's Day.

As we marveled at the connections she was making, we noticed the way in which Cathy was playing both inside and outside the changes in her own unique song—that same tune my other client, Ben, said we are all playing.

We found out together that Cathy could go into all sorts of conventional and unconventional ways of reading the harmonies of her constantly shifting emotional and intellectual chords, noticing the subtleties of sadness, pride, loss, and desire. For moments, it might seem to the casual observer that Cathy was losing her place in the song, as if she was getting it all wrong, but no, like a jazz soloist she was in full command of the changes and gathering more and more freedom to explore the nuance and complexity of all that she was now hearing in the moment.

Like a winding and weaving jazz saxophone solo, she was juxtaposing elements from the present and the past in more interesting and embellished variations and, in so doing, deepening her interpretation of her own special song.

As therapist, I was there as listener, accompanist, and collaborator, like a pianist in the rhythm section who picks up on a motif or chord in the soloist, and echoes it back for more exposition. At other times, with a nod or a gentle "yes," you could almost hear me laying back with the soft chimes of chords in the high registers, underscoring her birdlike flight in the foreground.

It was not lost on either of us the corrective emotional experience she was having sharing these new changes with a male figure who could not only see her equality but also could speak forcefully against the injustices of her me-too experience. It was especially gratifying that we could see this as a deeper way of reading the changes and becoming more free and discriminating in how to work new material into this unique song of hers.

At the end of the session, we joked about how we had done a new collaboration on a fantastic recording together, and that I was happy to be a sideman in her band.

With cheeky pride and playful tenderness, Cathy quipped, "We should keep this recording to ourselves. We don't want to break the internet by dropping this one on Spotify!" And I agreed—we had read and followed the changes together to places unimaginable only weeks and months before, and we were the witnesses of this wonderful music. We both knew we had found Cathy's special lead sheet. And no one could take it away from her anymore!

The Art of Disciplined Spontaneity

We don't often talk about the ingenious, resourceful, and elegant ways in which the psyche expresses, contains, and regulates itself, nor the ways in which within its so-called problems are also the seeds of its own healing, as Carl Jung taught. Once we become more tuned in, present, and discriminating, it is easy to see the masterful ways in which the psyche attempts to both make and avoid something creative. Making those connections is the artistic method of therapists as—to quote novelist Jhumpa Lahiri (1999)—"interpreters of maladies," the special power and gift we develop to both unpack and synthesize the range of our patients' full human condition and, in so doing, to help them transcend it.

Therapy is the art of capitalizing on disciplined spontaneity to make more interesting music and art together. It is the educational experience of teaching our clients how to incorporate an improvisational and artistic process into their personal, professional, and artistic lives. The psyche moves so fast but so expertly and wisely amid the many melodies and harmonies that we are meant to play. Unfortunately, without proper support and guidance, we have difficulty making music out of it, getting thrown off by the dissonances rather than learning how to embrace them and the many new and interesting territories they are trying to take us into.

Like metaphor itself, therapeutic improvisation isn't so much a frill as a way of thinking, feeling, and deeply engaging the vast material of our clients (Lakoff & Johnson, 1980). And unexpectedly enough, it has become a part of a revolutionary way of reimagining how the fields of interpersonal neurobiology, relational psychoanalysis, and psychotherapy outcome research overlap, synergize, and cross-pollinate.

In his 1970 national bestseller *The Man Who Mistook His Wife for a Hat*, Oliver Sacks (1990) foresaw this new hybrid between our problems and our possibilities, saying, "the study of disease and of identity cannot be disjoined. Such disorders, and their depiction and study indeed entail a new discipline, which we may call the 'neurology of identity,' for it deals with the neural foundations of the self." This work has been carried forward and expanded by a unique collection of interpersonal neurobiologists, relational psychoanalysts, and psychotherapy outcome researchers.

Just as the Three B's—Bach, Beethoven, and Brahms—were pivotal in the development and evolution of classical music, a collection of interpersonal neurobiologists is central to the study of the creative mutual interplay that is therapeutic improvisation. Allan Schore is the Bach of interpersonal neurobiology, showcasing the fugue-like way multiplicity manifests itself through our relationships and how this strange polyphony originates in the constant oscillation between our two hemispheres. Joining him are relational analysts Philip Bromberg and Donnel Stern, who have exquisitely articulated the consonances and dissonances of a constantly moving and unfolding self, one that is as prone to being transported away by dissociation as by creative surprise.

Oliver Sacks figures as the Beethoven of interpersonal neurobiology, working with equal measures of scientific and romantic prowess to stretch the field to be more than it was before. Just as Beethoven used the newly developed piano as a colossal force to be reckoned with against the entire orchestra, Sacks took the power of narrative and clinical tales and wove them into intricate tapestries that he threaded through our synapses with the uncannily ordered elements of the periodic table.

Damasio, Siegel, and McGilchrist, as the Brahms contingent of this masterful trio, artfully balance the logic, order, and symmetry of classical neuroscience with the expressivity and emotion of a right-brained Romanticism, reminding us that the mindful feeling way has always been and will always be the source of individual and collective creativity and innovation.

The Supershrink Superpower

Psychotherapy outcome researchers, especially those tuned in to therapist responsiveness, are showcasing the true power and reach of therapeutic improvisation. With an impressive body of empirical work, they are reminding all therapists that, beyond theory and technique, this most musical process—finding the right intervention with the right person at the right time—drives therapeutic growth and creative transformation (Heinonen et al., 2010; Silberschatz, 2021; Watson, 2021). Therapeutic improvisation as finding this right beat is the hallmark feature of the most effective and multiculturally sensitive treatments, ones that embrace the full diversity of our individual, collective, and cultural identities.

Silberschatz (2021) did a study of so-called supershrinks (Ricks, 1974), therapists who consistently leave their comparable peers in the dust, showing results and outcomes that are often 10 times better than those of their less effective therapist peers (Okiishi et al., 2003). These therapists were able to quickly attend to and identify their clients' pathogenic beliefs and find new ways to disconfirm them and engage corrective emotional experiences with them, making unexpected and new musical moments that the patients all truly desired but didn't know how to play.

In the parlance of control-mastery theory, these therapists were pro-plan, meaning they could fully receive and implement the plan the patient hoped would creatively open up, solve, and revise their life story and could skillfully weave this into the therapy. Just like a therapist well versed in the scales and arpeggios of therapeutic improvisation, supershrinks employ a wide-ranging repertoire of interventions, tonal styles, and levels of engagement with their patients.

One supershrink, for example, could switch between a highly active interpretive approach with a patient who felt guilt at surpassing her siblings and a more passive and listening stance with a patient raised by highly intrusive parents, who needed time and space to figure things out for himself. Another supershrink could toggle between giving ample reassurance, affection, and comfort to a mistreated patient who had unconsciously identified with being unworthy to being highly confrontational and reassuringly helpful with a patient who grew up in a family with entrenched and pervasive denial that left them completely on their own to become self-destructive and in denial themselves. This selfsame therapist, like a good accompanist playing more softly, could flexibly provide more tender and loving self-compassion and support to a highly self-critical and punitive client so that the beauty of their own music could be heard yet again.

These supershrinks were rightfully perceived as the most responsive to their clients, engaging in a depth of creative interplay that not only witnessed and recognized past grievances but also actively rewrote the story. To echo poet laureate Billy Collins (1999), they are helping their patients transform the biography "they are reading and writing simultaneously in a language troublesome and private" into one that is shared and expansive.

How might we understand the superpowers of these supershrinks in the language of therapeutic improvisation? These therapists are highly tuned through their therapeutic presence in order to accurately hear and synthesize their clients' main problems, conflicts, and dilemmas, and use their honed-in therapeutic authority to establish a new formulation in changing clients' understanding of their situation and living it out with them in tests and disconfirmation in the relationship itself.

When we have full and regular access to our multiplicity—the diverse and elaborate cast of characters inside of ourselves—and we use it in a state of perpetual responsiveness to ourselves and others, we are in an ongoing process of optimal mental health. Tapped into an integrated, holistic, and elaborated connection to ourselves and the world, we tap into a portable flow state that is mindful, grounded, and fluid. And what is better yet, we become exquisitely alert to and intrigued by the possibilities and opportunities that minor and major adjustments can make in an ongoing creative dialogue with ourselves, others, and the world. Like Stefon Harris's jazz player on the bandstand, we don't get bogged down in mistakes, but instead become more and more aware of the microshifts that we can play into new territory together. Like Goethe, we become much more intrigued by this liquid architecture.

Staying Present in a World of Disconnection

In a world where conversation is flattening and degenerating, where our attention spans have shrunk to less than those of goldfishes, we are in ever need of maintaining presence and purpose. MIT clinical psychologist and sociologist Sherry Turkle (2021) talks and writes widely about the loss we are all feeling with adapting our new technologies to our oldest technologies: the joint arts of empathy, creativity, and connection. For her, empathy is "the ability not only to put yourself in someone else's place, but to put yourself in someone else's problem" (Turkle, 2021). Again, it's a way of getting comfortable with the dissonances and learning the dynamic interplay of making ourselves curious and available again.

Therapeutic improvisation is going to continue to become more and more important as a way of safeguarding, honoring, and transmitting not just our clinical know-how but the essence of what it is to be fully human, alive, and creative. And the more we can own that in ourselves, the more we can share it with our clients and bring a whole new music to the world.

TED TIE-INS

INTRODUCTION: From Winging It to Owning It

Chimamanda Ngozie Adichie: The Danger of a Single Story. A novelist looks at the ways we can so easily pigeonhole and typecast each other, foreclosing the possibilities of honoring and respecting the diversity of our human multiplicity.

Stefon Harris: There Are No Mistakes on the Bandstand. A jazz vibraphonist shows us that improvisation is much more than we think it truly is, a profound experience of listening and responding deeply as we do in our most creative therapeutic moments.

CHAPTER 1: Is This Thing On? Finding Your Voice

Sir Ken Robinson: Do Schools Kill Creativity? A prolific writer and speaker on education, Sir Ken Robinson inspires us to reimagine how schools can help us maintain our creativity and the many ways in which they unintentionally harm us.

Elizabeth Gilbert: Your Elusive Creative Genius. A journalist and writer flips the script on our beliefs about artists, showing that instead of there just being that rare genius outside of us, we all have a genius inside of us.

Adam Grant: Original Thinkers. An organizational psychologist examines the habits of original thinkers and opens up a window into the psychological process of creative improvisation.

CHAPTER 2: Righting the Left Brain: Neuroscience Makes Artists Out of Us

Dan Siegel: Mindfulness and Neural Integration. A psychiatrist and neuroscientist teaches us about the interconnections of the brain and its miraculous impact on self-regulation, connection, and well-being.

Antonio Damasio: The Quest to Understand Consciousness. A neuroscientist explains how our brain creates a sense of self and untangles the mysteries of consciousness.

Lisa Feldman Barrett: You Aren't at the Mercy of Your Emotions. A brain researcher explains how our emotions really work and how we might actually have some control over them.

CHAPTER 3: Weaving Together Many Voices: Therapeutic Polyphony

Roger Evernden: Becoming Your Many Selves. A business architect, Evernden illuminates the many aspects of self that most of us miss inhabiting and shows us how by embracing them we can be the best version of ourselves and honor our true diversity.

Dan Gilbert: The Psychology of Your Future Self. A Harvard social psychologist shows us how easily we all misjudge our concept of ourselves and time, and that we are all much more fluid than we realize.

CHAPTER 4: Therapeutic Presence: Not-Knowing and Staying Tuned In

Julian Treasure: How to Listen Better. A sound engineer teaches us five ways to tune our ears, reinforcing our emerging skills in being more therapeutically present.

Andy Petticombe: All It Takes Is 10 Mindful Minutes. A mindfulness expert shows you how to capitalize on just 10 minutes to help you get more tuned and present for your day and work as a therapist.

CHAPTER 5: Therapeutic Authority: Owning Your Confidence and Making Music

Itay Talgam: Lead Like the Great Conductors. A world-class violinist and conductor beautifully demonstrates how to integrate therapeutic presence and authority, replete with vivid illustrations of conductors showing the analogues in music.

CHAPTER 6: Why You Need Lateral Mentors Too

Bob McKinnon: How Did You End Up Here? Dream Teams and Tailwinds. A media studies professor and social justice change maker shows us how to make the most out of our mentors and use them as our own dream team.

Deborah Heiser: Rethinking Aging: Mentoring a New Generation. A developmental psychologist helps us reimagine the ways we think about mentoring and generativity and their connection to maintaining fulfillment, creativity, and connection through the life span.

CHAPTER 7: Toward a New Vision of Mental Health

Martin Seligman: The New Era of Positive Psychology. A pioneering psychology professor, researcher, and writer explores what is good about psychology, what is not good about psychology, and what we can do to make it good enough and even better.

Mihaly Csikszentmihalyi: Flow, the Secret to Happiness. Another pioneering psychology professor on creativity, happiness, and fulfillment explores how and why the flow state contributes to a life worth living.

BIBLIOGRAPHY

Adichie, C. N. (2009). *The danger of a single story* [Video]. Ted Conferences. https://www.ted.com/talks/chimamanda_ngozi_adichie_
the_danger_of_a_single_story?language=en

Alcée, M. (2017). *Introverts, college, and the mind: Solving our mental health crisis* [Video]. TEDx Talks. https://www.youtube.com/
watch?v=vkkGPyc3ZmA

Alcée, M. D., & Sager, T. A. (2017). How to fall in love with time-limited therapy: Lessons from poetry and music. *Journal of College Student Psychotherapy, 31*(3), 203–214. doi:10.1080/875682
25.2016.1276420

Aron, E. N. (1996). *The highly sensitive person.* New York: Broadway.

Bach, J. S. (1997). *The well-tempered clavier. Book I: 24 preludes and fugues, BWV, 846–857.* Munich: Naxos.

Barry, E. (1972). *Robert Frost on writing.* New Brunswick, NJ: Rutgers University Press.

Beethoven, L. V. (1996). *Symphony no. 5 in C minor, Op. 67, allegro con brio* [Recorded by Carlos Kleiber and the Weiner Philharmoniker]. On *Beethoven: Symphonies 5 and 7* [CD]. Berlin: Deutsche Gramophon. (Original work published 1808)

Bollas, C. (2015). *Being a character: Psychoanalysis and self experience.* Routledge.

Bowie, D. (1971). Changes [Song]. On *Hunky Dory.* RCA.

Bowlby, J. (1969). *Attachment and loss: Vol. 1. Attachment*. New York: Basic Books.

Boyce, W. T. (2019). *The orchid and the dandelion: Why some children struggle and how all can thrive*. Bluebird.

Bradbury, R. (1990). *Zen in the art of writing*. Santa Barbara, CA: Joshua Odell.

Breuer, J., & Freud, S. (2000). *Studies on Hysteria*. New York: Basic Books.

Bromberg, P. M. (2006). *Awakening the dreamer: Clinical journeys*, Mahwah, NJ: Analytic Press. doi:10.4324/9780203759981

Bromberg, P.M. (2011). *The shadow of the tsunami and the growth of the relational mind*. New York, NY: Routledge.

Buber, M. (1958). *I and thou* (2nd ed.). New York, NY: Scribner.

Cain, S. (2013). *Quiet: The power of introverts in a world that can't stop talking*. London: Penguin.

Cameron, J. (1992). *The artist's way: A spiritual path to higher creativity*. Los Angeles: Jeremy P. Tarcher/Perigee.

Canning, I., Sherman, E., Unwith, G., (Producers) & Hooper, T. (Directors). (2010) The King's Speech [Motion Picture]. UK: Momentum Pictures.

Carlile, B., Hanseroth, P., & Hanseroth, T. (2018). The Mother [Brandi Carlile] On By the way, I forgive you [LP]. Nashville, TN: Elektra.

Carnegie, D. (1964). How to win friends and influence people. New York: Simon and Schuster.

Carver, R. (2009). *What we talk about when we talk about love*. London: Vintage.

Chow, D. L., Miller, S. D., Seidel, J. A., Kane, R. T., Thornton, J. A., & Andrews, W. P. (2015). The role of deliberate practice in the development of highly effective psychotherapists, *Psychotherapy*, *52*(3), 337–345. https://doi.org/10.1037/pst0000015

Cohen, Leonard (1992). Anthem [Recorded by Leonard Cohen] On The Future [LP] Columbia.

Coles, R. (1989). *The call of stories: Teaching and the moral imagination*. Boston: Houghton Mifflin.

Collins, B. (1995). Nightclub. In *The art of drowning* (pp. 92–93). Pittsburgh: University of Pittsburgh Press.

Collins, B. (1999). Cliché. In *Questions about angels* (p. 43). Pittsburgh: University of Pittsburgh Press.

Coltrane, J. (1964). *Bessie's blues* [CD]. Crescent.

Coltrane, J. (1976). *Giant steps* [CD]. WEA-Musik.

Corbett, R. (2016). *You must change your life: The story of Rainer Maria Rilke and Auguste Rodin.* New York: Norton.

Cornford, F. D. (1965). *Collected poems.* London: Cresset.

Cozolino, L. (2004). *The making of a therapist.* New York: Norton.

Damasio, A. R. (2019). *The strange order of things: Life, feeling, and the making of cultures.* New York: Vintage.

da Vinci, L. (1490). *Vitruvian Man* [Pen and ink with wash over metalpoint on paper]. Gallerie dell'Accademica, Venice.

Davis, M. (1959). *Kind of blue* [CD]. Columbia/Legacy.

Dickinson, E. (1976a). Poem 314. In T. H. Johnson (Ed.), *The complete poems of Emily Dickinson.* Boston: Little, Brown.

Dickinson, E. (1976b). Poem 466. In T. H. Johnson (Ed.), *The complete poems of Emily Dickinson.* Boston: Little, Brown.

Docter, P., & Del Carmen, R. (2015). *Inside out.* Walt Disney Studios Motion Pictures.

Dunn, J. (2017). *How not to hate your husband after kids.* New York: Little, Brown.

Dweck, C. S. (2008). Mindset: The new psychology of success. New York, NY: Ballantine Books.

Engel, S. (2015). *The hungry mind: The origins of curiosity in childhood.* Cambridge, MA: Harvard University Press.

Engel, S. (2021). *The intellectual lives of children.* Cambridge, MA: Harvard University Press.

Epstein, D. (2019). *Range: Why generalists triumph in a specialized world.* New York: Riverhead.

Ericsson, A., Pool, R., & Beevers, G. (2016). *Peak: Secrets from the new science of expertise.* London: Random House.

Erikson, E. & Coles, R. (2000). *The Erik Erikson Reader.* New York: Norton.

Faris, V., & Dayton, J. (2006). *Little Miss Sunshine* [Film]. Fox Searchlight Pictures.

Fawcett, A. (1978). *California rock, California sound.* Los Angeles: Reed Books.

Friedlander, M. L. (2012). Therapist responsiveness: Mirrored in supervisor responsiveness. *Clinical Supervisor, 31*(1), 103–119.

Friedlander, M. (2015). Use of relational strategies to repair alliance ruptures: How responsive supervisors train responsive psychotherapists. *Psychotherapy, 52*(2), 174–179.

Freud, S., & Gay, P. (1995). *The Freud reader.* London: Vintage.

Fromm, E. (1956). *The art of loving.* New York: Harper.

Frost, R. (1931) "Education by Poetry." *Amherst Graduates' Quarterly.*

Frost, R. (1939). The Figure a Poem Makes. In *Collected poems of Robert Frost.* New York: Holt, Rinehart, and Winston.

Frost, R. (1991). *The road not taken: A selection of Robert Frost's poems.* New York: H. Holt and Co.

Geller, S. M., & Greenberg, L. S. (2012). *Therapeutic presence: A mindful approach to effective therapy.* Washington, DC: American Psychological Association.

Gilbert, J. (2005). Failing and Falling. In *Refusing heaven* (p. 18). New York: Alfred A. Knopf.

Gladwell, M. (2005). *Blink: The power of thinking without thinking.* Boston: Little, Brown.

Golding, W. (1954). *Lord of the flies.* New York: Perigee.

Gondry, M. (2004). *Eternal sunshine of the spotless mind* [Film]. Focus Features.

Gottman, J. M., & Silver, N. (1999). *The seven principles for making marriage work.* New York: Three Rivers.

Grant, A. M. (2013). Rethinking the extraverted sales ideal. *Psychological Science, 24*(6), 1024–1030. doi:10.1177/0956797612463706

Grant, A. (2016). *Originals: How non-conformists move the world.* New York: Viking.

Grayson, P. A. (2002). Psychodynamic psychotherapy with undergraduate and graduate students. In F. W. Kaslow & J. J. Magnavita (Eds.), *Comprehensive handbook of psychotherapy: Vol. 1. Psychodynamic/object relations* (pp. 161–179). New York: John Wiley.

Harris, S. (2011). *There are no mistakes on the bandstand* [Video]. TED Conferences. https://www.ted.com/talks/stefon_harris_there_are_no_mistakes_on_the_bandstand/up-next?language+en

Hart, A. (2003). What do entanglements reveal about the analytic role? A clinical communication from consulting room and college counseling service. *Psychoanalytic Review, 90*(3). https://doi.org/10.1521/prev.90.3.329.23618

Hart, A. (2020). Principles for teaching diversity in a psychoanalytic context. *Contemporary Psychoanalysis, 56*(2–3), 404–417.

Hasse, J. E. (1995). *Beyond category: The life and genius of Duke Ellington.* New York: Da Capo.

Hatcher, R. (2015). Interpersonal competencies: Responsiveness, technique, and training in psychotherapy. *American Psychologist, 70*(8), 747–757. https://doi.org/10.1037/a0039803

Heinonen, E., Lindfors, O., Laaksonen, M., & Knekt, P. (2012). Therapists' professional and personal characteristics as predictors of outcome in short- and long-term psychotherapy. *Journal of Affective Disorders, 138*, 301–312. doi:10.1016/j.jad.2012.01.023

Heiser, D. (2020, July 16). Lateral mentors: your next mentor might be sitting right next to you. *The Right Side of 40.* https://www.psychologytoday.com/us/blog/the-right-side-40/202007/lateral-mentors

Herman, J. (1997). *Trauma and recovery: The aftermath of violence—from domestic abuse to political terror.* New York: Basic Books.

Hoagland, T. (1998). Totally. In *Donkey gospel* (pp. 70–71). Graywolf Press.

Howard, R. (2001). *A beautiful mind* [Film]. Universal Pictures.

Hunstein, D. (2017, March 25). *Miles Davis and John Coltrane, 1959* [Photo]. In C. Guise, Don Hunstein remembered. Rockarchive. https://www.rockarchive.com/news/2017/don-hunstein-remembered (Original work published 1959)

Huxley, A. (1932). *Brave new world.* New York: Harper Brothers.

Jung, C. G. (1933). *Modern man in search of a soul.* New York: Harcourt, Brace & World.

Jung, C. G. (2014). Psychological aspects of the mother archetype. In Jung, C. G., Adler, G., & Hull, R. F. C. (Eds.). *Collected works of*

C.G. Jung, Volume 9 (Part 1): Archetypes and the Collective Uncon-scious, p. 172. Princeton, NJ: Princeton University Press.

Kabat-Zinn, J. (2019). *The healing power of mindfulness: A new way of being*. Boston: Little, Brown.

Kagan, J., & Snidman, N. (2004). *The long shadow of temperament*. Cambridge, MA: Harvard University Press.

Kalsched, D. (1996). *The inner world of trauma: Archetypal defense of the personal spirit*. London: Routledge.

Kalsched, D. (2013). *Trauma and the soul: A psycho-spiritual approach to human development*. East Sussex, UK: Routledge.

Kerouac, J. (2018). *On the road*. London: Penguin.

Kershner, I., & Lucas, G. (1980). *The empire strikes back* [Film]. Twen-tieth Century Fox Film Corporation.

Kincaid, J. (1991). On seeing England for the first time. *Transition*, *51*(19910101), pp. 32–40.

Klein, A. (2018, January 8). A sexist troll attacked Sara Silverman. She responded by helping him with his problems. *Washing-ton Post*. https://www.washingtonpost.com/news/inspired-life/wp/2018/01/08/a-man-trolled-sarah-silverman-on-twitter-she-ended-up-helping-him-with-his-medical-problems/

Knoblauch, S. H. (2000). *The musical edge of therapeutic dialogue*. Hillsdale, NJ: The Analytic Press.

Kornfield, J. & Khechog, N. (2001). *Meditation for beginners*. Boulder, Co: Sounds True Audio.

Lahiri, J. (1999). *Interpreter of maladies*. New York: Mariner-Houghton.

Lakoff, G., & Johnson, M. (1980). Metaphors we live by. University of Chicago Press.

Langer, E. J. (1997). *The power of mindful learning*. Cambridge, MA: Perseus.

Langer, E. J. (2005). *On becoming an artist: Reinventing yourself through mindful creativity*. New York: Ballantine.

Lee, H. (2006). *To kill a mockingbird*. New York: Harper Perennial Modern Classics.

Lee, S., & Blanchard, T. (2002). *25th hour* [Film]. Buena Vista Pictures.

Lehrer, J. (2008). *Proust was a neuroscientist*. New York: Mariner.

Levenson, H. (2010). *Brief dynamic therapy.* Washington, DC: American Psychological Association.

Levenson, H. (2021, March 5). Deliberate practice. Presented to the San Francisco Psychotherapy Research Group, Virtual Conference.

Lewin, R. (1997). *Creative collaboration in psychotherapy: Making room for life.* Northvale, NJ: Jason Aronson.

Martin, J. L., Hess, T. R., Ain, S. C., Nelson, D. L., & Locke, B. D. (2012). Collecting multidimensional client data using repeated measures: Experiences of clients and counselors using the CCAPS-34. *Journal of College Counseling, 15*(3), 247–261. doi:10.1002/j.2161-1882.2012.00019.x

Mattheson, R. & Simmons, R. (1957). *The incredible shrinking man.* Universal Pictures.

May, R. (1994). *The courage to create.* New York: Norton.

McGilchrist, I. (2009). *The master and his emissary: The divided brain and the making of the Western world.* New Haven, CT: Yale University Press.

McKinnon, B. (2018). How did you end up here? Dream teams and tailwinds. [Video File]. Ted Conferences. Retrieved from:https://www.ted.com/talks/bob_mckinnon_how_did_you_end_up_here_dream_teams_tailwinds

McKinnon, B. (2021). *Three little engines.* Grosset & Dunlap.

McWilliams, N. (1999). *Psychoanalytic case conceptualization.* New York: Guilford.

Mitchell, J. (1971). A case of you [Song]. On *Blue.* Reprise.

Mitchell, S. (1988). *Relational concepts in psychoanalysis: An integration.* Cambridge, MA: Harvard University Press.

Neruda, P. (2015). *The poetry of Pablo Neruda.* New York: Farrar, Straus, & Giroux.

Neville, M., Capotosto, C., & Ma, N. (2018). *Won't you be my neighbor?* [Film]. Focus Features.

Ogden, T. (1997). Reverie and metaphor: Some thoughts on how I work as a psychoanalyst. *International Journal of Psychoanalysis, 78,* 719–732.

Pink, D. H. (2012). *To sell is human: The surprising truth about moving others.* New York: Riverhead Books.

Pink, D. H. (2006). *A whole new mind: Why right-brainers will rule the future*. London: Cyan.

Rachmaninov, S. (1973). *Symphony in E minor, Op. 27* [Recorded by Leonard Slatkin & the Detroit Symphony Orchestra]. On *Rachmaninov: Symphony No. 2*. Hong Kong: Naxos. (Original work published 1908)

Rilke, R. M. (1992). *Letters to a young poet*. San Rafael, CA: New World Library.

Robertson, C. (1997). *The dictionary of quotations*. Hertfordshire, UK: Wordsworthy Editions.

Rock, M. H. (1997). *Psychodynamic supervision: Perspectives of the supervisor and the supervisee*. Northvale, NJ: Jason Aronson.

Ronson, J. (2015). *So you've been publicly shamed*. New York: Riverhead.

Rousmaniere, T. (2016). *Deliberate practice for psychotherapists: A guide to improving clinical effectiveness*. New York: Routledge.

Rousmaniere, T., Goodyear, R. K., Miller, S. D., & Wampold, B. E. (2016). *The cycle of excellence: Using deliberate practice to improve supervision and training*. Hoboken, NJ: John Wiley.

Rowling, J. K. (1999). *Harry Potter and the sorcerer's stone*. New York: Scholastic.

Rubin, J. B. (2011). *The art of flourishing: A new East-West approach to staying sane and finding love in an insane world*. New York: Random House.

Rūmī, J. A.-D., & Washington, P. (2006). *Rumi: Poems*. New York: Alfred A. Knopf.

Russel, D. O., Davis, J., Ellison, M., Gordon, J., & Mok, K. (2015). *Joy* [Film]. Twentieth Century Fox.

Sacks, O. (1990). *The man who mistook his wife for a hat and other clinical tales*. New York: Harper Perennial.

Sacks, O. (2018). *The river of consciousness*. New York: Vintage Books.

Saint-Exupéry, A. D., & Testot-Ferry, I. (2018). *The little prince*. Ware, UK: Wordsworth Editions.

Schore, A. N. (2019). *Right brain psychotherapy*. New York: Norton.

Schutz, L. E. (2005). Broad-perspective perceptual disorder of the right hemisphere. *Neuropsychology Review, 15*, 11–27.

Schwartz, M. (2017). *The possibility principle: How quantum physics can improve the way you think, live, and love.* Boulder, CO: Sounds True.

Schwartzman, J., Williams, O., Murray, B., & Anderson, W. (1999). *Rushmore* [Film]. Irvington, NY: Criterion Collection.

Sendak, M. (1984). *Where the wild things are.* New York: Harper and Row.

Shaffer, P. (1973). *Equus: A play.* London: Samuel French.

Shakespeare, W. (2002). Sonnet 18. In C. Burrow (Ed.), *The complete sonnets and poems.* New York: Oxford University Press.

Shakespeare, W. (2015). *The collected works of William Shakespeare.* Dammweg: Pergamonmedia.

Siegel, D. J. (2010). *Mindsight: The new science of personal transformation.* New York: Bantam.

Siegel, D. J., & Bryson, T. P. (2012). *The whole-brain child: 12 revolutionary strategies to nurture your child's developing mind.* New York: Bantam.

Silberschatz, G. (2021). Responsiveness in control-mastery theory. In J. C. Watson & H. Wisemen (Eds.), *The responsive psychotherapist: Attuning to clients in the moment.* Washington, DC: American Psychological Association.

Soong, K. (2017, September 20). How a Black Lives Matter activist took the stage and got Trump supporters to listen at last weekend's DC rally. *Washington Post.* https://www.washingtonpost.com/news/inspired-life/wp/2017/09/20/how-a-black-lives-matter-activist-took-the-stage-and-got-trump-supporters-to-listen-at-last-weekends-dc-rally/

Stern, D. B. (2009). *Partners in thought: Working with unformulated experience, dissociation, and enactment.* New York: Routledge.

Stern, D. B. (2017). Courting surprise. In D. B. Stern & I. Hirsch (Eds.), *The interpersonal perspective in psychoanalysis, 1960s–1990s* (pp. 252–253). New York: Routledge. doi:10.4324/9781315471976-2

Sullivan, H. S. (1954). *The psychiatric interview.* New York: Norton.

Szymborska, W., Barańczak, S., & Cavanagh, C. (2000). *Poems, new and collected, 1957–1997.* San Diego: Harcourt Brace.

Talgam, I. (2009). *Lead like the great conductors* [Video]. TED Con-

ferences. https://www.ted.com/talks/itay_talgam_lead_like_the_
great_conductors?language=en

Thomas, E., Ryder, A., & Nolan, C .(2006). *The prestige* [Motion Picture] US/UK: Buena Vista Pictures.

Tocqueville, A., Mansfield, H. C., & Winthrop, D. (2000). *Democracy in America*. Chicago: University of Chicago Press.

Turkle, S. (2021). *The empathy diaries: a memoir*. New York: Penguin Press.

Van Sant, G. (1997). *Good will hunting* [Film]. Miramax.

Vaughan, S., Eckstine, B., Treadwell, G., Monney, H., & Jones, Q. (2000). The nearness of you [Song]. On *Sarah Vaughan: Ken Burns jazz* [CD]. Verve.

Wachtel, P. (1993). *Therapeutic communication: Knowing what to say when*. New York: Guilford.

Wampold, B. E. (2001) *The great psychotherapy debate: Models, methods, and findings*. New York: Routledge.

Watson, J. C. (2021). Responsiveness in emotion-centered therapy. In J. C. Watson & H. Wisemen (Eds.), *The responsive psychotherapist: Attuning to clients in the moment*. Washington, DC: American Psychological Association.

Whitman, W. (1997). *Leaves of grass: Selected poems and prose*. New York: Doubleday.

Wilde, O. (2017). *The importance of being earnest and other plays*. London: Macmillan Collectors Library.

Wilder, T. (2015). *The bridge of San Luis Rey*. New York: Harper Perennial.

Williams, T. (1999). *The glass menagerie*. New York: New Directions.

Winnicott, D. W. (2016). *Through paediatrics to psycho-analysis: Collected papers*. London: Routledge.

Yalom, I. (2002). *The gift of therapy: An open letter to a new generation of therapists and their patients*. New York: Harper Collins.

Yalom, I. D., & Leszcz, M. (2005). *The theory and practice of group psychotherapy*. New York: Basic Books.

Yan, W. J., Wu, Q., Liang, J., Chen, Y. H., and Fu, X. (2013). How fast are the leaked facial expressions: the duration of micro-expres-

sions. *Journal of Nonverbal Behavior. 37*, 217–230. doi:10.1007/
s10919-013-0159-8.

Zemeckis, R. (2000). *Cast away.* Twentieth Century Fox.

INDEX

ABOUT THE AUTHOR

Michael Alcée, PhD, is a clinical psychologist in private practice in Tarrytown, NY, and Mental Health Educator at Manhattan School of Music. He specializes in the psychology of artists, as well as the everyday creativity and professional development of therapists. He has worked in college counseling at Fordham University and Vassar College and was Training Coordinator at the counseling center at Ramapo College of New Jersey.

He won the American Psychological Association's 2019 Schillinger Memorial prize for his essay on the link between jazz and psychoanalysis titled, "Reading the Changes: Freud's Improvisational Art." In being awarded first prize by Division 39, his essay was called a "truly dazzling tour de force."

His contributions have appeared in *The Chicago Tribune*, the *New York Times*, NPR, Salon.com, and on the TEDx stage. He inspires therapists and nontherapists alike to *Live Life Creatively* on his selfsame titled podcast and Psychology Today blog.